A WOR DIFFERENCE
THE BIG GREEN POETRY MACHINE

Recycle, Recycle, Recycle! Love the world you live in. Be good to your planet. Don't be mean, be green! Recycle, Recycle, Recycle! Love the world you live in. Be good to your planet. Don't be mean, be green! Recycle, Recycle, Recycle! Love the world you live in. Be good to your planet. Don't be mean, be green! Recycle, Recycle, Recycle! Love the

West Midlands Poets
Edited by Annabel Cook

First published in Great Britain in 2009 by:

 Young**Writers**

Young Writers
Remus House
Coltsfoot Drive
Peterborough
PE2 9JX
Telephone: 01733 890066
Website: www.youngwriters.co.uk

Foreword

Young Writers' A World of Difference is a showcase for our nation's most brilliant young poets to share their thoughts, hopes and fears for the planet they call home.

Young Writers was established in 1990 to nurture creativity in our children and young adults, to give them an interest in poetry and an outlet to express themselves. Seeing their work in print will encourage them to keep writing as they grow, and become our poets of tomorrow.

Selecting the poems has been challenging and immensely rewarding. The effort and imagination invested by these young writers makes their poems a pleasure to enjoy reading time and time again.

Contents

Hodge Hill Sports & Enterprise College

Holyhead School

King Edward VI Five Ways School

Lyndon School

The Poems

Without The Planet We Would Not Exist

As I watched down from the ashy clouds
A thought struck my mind, day and night
The planet transforms itself to be in inferior situations
Why? I did not understand
I learnt through experience and realised
The planet needs caring but
It has never crossed several minds.

Free the world from its milieu
Deep thoughts flutter across minds
Assessing the world but don't know what to do
Glancing around, what do you see?
Contaminated globe, mucky concrete
Polluted air, famished homeless,
Inconsiderate wars, racial discrimination . . .

The sphere globe shouts for facilitate
But no one seems to hear, defend ears, and blinded eyes,
The nation is not in its right mind
The ecosystem is as not friendly as it seems
Battered, cold, not bothered for, even though
Without the world there would be no one
Has it yet frustrated anyone's mind?

Free the world from poverty
Help a child in the Third World countries, join a charitable trust
Unpolluted the firmament, tyres may be fast but feet are harmless
Clean the streets, don't let rubbish ruin a safer planet
Recycle, save trees and you'll be on
Top of the list for living longer
Oxygen we need, and trees are delighted to provide us with it.

What's more important paper or to live?
Trees cut down yelling 'No!' one tree down, no motion
Cultures daunt at each other with judgements
Unpleasant words wing to each other, batted back with no regret
Nature ruined, habitats murdered
How would you feel without a home just like the animals?
So be positive and do something for the Earth.

Wind back 10 years ago
Mankind was appreciated
Blue skies were cleaner than ever, fresh fragrant
Flowers lived longer, wide opening their petals

Animals sang for pleasure
Smile on every species
No worry, no pain
The world was at peace at last
Isn't this more like what we want now?

Be kind and rescue the planet
Then you'll be known as a hero
The world's full of meaning but
Various don't comprehend, one day
They'll think back and review their errors.
Others will be proud, with their head help up high
Glad to save the world and live a better life.

Situations can change at any time
It is not as hard as it sounds,
Just have faith and succeed.
The world would end
Without it being cared for.
So think for a second
And decide what you want to do.

Hamida Bi (14)
Bordesley Green Girls' School

Eco-Poem

This is my eco-poem,
We don't know where it's snowing,
The ice caps are melting,
That's what we are shouting,
Save the Earth,
We're heating up Earth,
By laying too much turf,
Our cars' engines are roaring,
Petrol prices are soaring,
Save the Earth,
Although the facts are boring,
We shouldn't be ignoring,
Don't sit there yawning,
Save the Earth.

Myles Deacon (11)
Caludon Castle School

Make The Solution

We've got the pollution, have you got the solution,
Stop cutting down trees, you'll be the bees' knees.

Save the crap, make up a rap,
Stop the pollution, it's the solution,
Turn off the standby, save the world,
Keep it with you, let it stick like glue.

So recycle bottles, recycle cans,
Don't let them be like lorries and vans,
Recycle is the solution,
Please stop the pollution.

Cut down on driving, it's a bit like dividing,
Only you half the petrol you use,
Cut down on pollution, it's the solution,
Don't smoke or others will choke,
It's no joke, cut down the smoke,
Stop the pollution is the solution.

Don't do the crime if you can't do the time
Don't drop litter, it's just bitter,
So put it in the bin, go and do a sin,
Don't drop litter is the solution,
So do something about the pollution.

Global warming is getting near,
Maybe your children won't know a deer,
So save the world for my sake and yours,
But for the next generation as well,
So stop the pollution is the solution.

Stop putting the heater on,
It's costing the Earth, put on a jumper,
Or play on the astro turf so
Don't waste electric, is the solution,
Please stop the pollution, pollution, pollution.

Shannon Stanley (11)
Caludon Castle School

3

You Can Help!

I always got the same old thing,
Of course it had to be Mum,
'Come down now and recycle your paper!'
'Oh my gosh, I'll do it later!'

Yes, yes, yes,
I know it's bad,
But don't blame me,
I'm not that sad.

Paper, cardboard,
Things like that,
Yes I do know,
It's not that phat.

There's other things,
There really is,
Like gas and transport,
I've taken the quiz,
Even more boring isn't it?
There really is so much more.

But then I realised,
I finally did,
I was looking in the shops,
Then bumped into Sid.

He told me all these dreadful things,
Like trees falling down,
Petrol polluting, up in the air,
If I didn't sort this out quick enough,
We wouldn't have enough
To go to the fair.

I thought again,
And took one last look,
No more TV,
Just read a book.

How can I make this even better now?
I don't know, go to town?
No, I can do much better,
How about I write a letter?

Yes, yes, yes, that's fantastic,
I'll write it about something great,

Like the Earth,
And its environment,
I'm bound to get a new mate.

I was saving money,
Just like that,
Buying this,
And buying that.

I liked this once I tried it,
It was cool,
But I knew the kids would say,
'Too cool for school!'

But I don't care,
What they say,
One day they'll have to pay,
But if they don't follow these rules,
They won't be getting all these jewels.

I was lying on my bed,
Wondering how I could make everybody understand,
I shot right up,
And thought about my land.

The next day I woke up,
Starting jotting all these little things down,
About the Earth and things like that.

Then I made a few posters,
Designed some leaflets,
Wrote out a speech,
All on scrap paper.

Made a great entrance, as I enter,
There I was in the middle of the centre,
Many people staring at me,
But I was feeling quite glee;
Read out my speech . . .
Threw out the leaflets . . .
Tossed over my posters . . .
They took a glance.

Everyone cheered!

Shakira Siddiqui (12)
Caludon Castle School

Environment Alert!

The environment, a dead list,
Predator warming the world,
How can we stop it or
Would the world fold?
There's a thing called war,
We can't just take it anymore.
Can't we just settle it,
The world will just become a large pit,
Soon the world will collide,
After that would there be anything to find?
Look at the world now in this condition,
Will it face the world 'extinction?'
Could you lesson your carbon footprint,
Or the world will be extinct.

Have you heart of the ozone,
It's slowly dying,
If you don't do something,
The sun will come to the Earth
And we will be frying,
Look at the cars releasing their smoke,
It is us to blame because we're
The ones who provoked it,
In 2010, will the world be the same?
If not, we will be the ones to blame,
Did you know the poles are thawing?
Have you ever heard of global warming?
Nothing will be left except the Earth's core,
No one will be able to live anymore,
Did you know the climate's changing?
Will it stop raining?
I hope this poem has change your opinion about the world,
If it hasn't, are you gonna let the world mould?

Jaskaran Singh Sembi (11)
Caludon Castle School

Be Green

Look at that rain,
It's a real pain,
That's global warming,
It's really storming.

The ice is melting,
The sun's really pelting,
The sun's getting hotter,
Nature's starting to totter.

Look at that litter,
It's really bitter,
Animals are dying,
God is crying.

Creatures are extinct,
Humans are linked,
Rivers and seas,
Are going like trees.

Look at the lake,
There's a lot at stake,
It's turning into water vapour,
It's going like paper.

Look at what we've done,
Our chances are none,
There's no turning back,
We are slack.

Children will die at thirteen,
Because of gasoline,
Nature's being mean,
Because we're not being
Green!

Aaron Comer (11)
Caludon Castle School

7

Racism

Racism is bad,
So stop it lad,
You don't know what it feels like,
Not to be white,
I know I'm black,
But I'm as friendly as you.

Racism is bad,
So stop it lad,
I have feelings,
Like everybody else,
My bones are broken,
Just like my heart,
You don't know how much it hurts,
So please stop racism,
Before it goes too far.

Racism is bad,
So stop it lad,
I'm going home,
Without a heart,
It's the end of the day,
To people I'm a monster,
But in what's left of my heart,
It's a pile of gold,
So stop it lad,
Let me say 'Hi!'

Kyle Patel (11)
Caludon Castle School

Litter!

L itter is bitter,
I t looks like glitter,
T itter? Don't titter, bin that litter!
T hrow litter in the bin, it's not hard to do!
E co squad save the world!
R ecycle plastic, it will be fantastic.

Demileigh Craven (11)
Caludon Castle School

A Greener World

A greener world,
A greener world,
It's what everybody
Dreams about.

A greener world,
A greener world,
It's what everybody
Talks about.

Yet no one ever
Stands up and says,
'I'm going to make a difference!
I'm going to do it whether you like it or not!
Our world deserves the best!'

They don't say,
'Hey kid put that in a bin!'
They just tut and walk on by.

Why can't people understand
The world is yours and mine.

Look after the world,
For it looks after us.

A greener world,
A greener world,
It's what we need!

Lewis Kimberley (11)
Caludon Castle School

War

W ar should be against the law!
A fter winning war, there is only more death,
R ight after the war, the world is really sore.

There should be no war!

Shaun Elliott-Jackson (12)
Caludon Castle School

Save Today, To Save Tomorrow

Save today, save tomorrow,
Help everyone here,
Otherwise you'll be in sorrow,
Don't just sit and have a beer.

Reduce your carbon footprint,
Reuse all your plastic bags,
Recycle all your paper prints,
Refuse all those fags.

Stop some of the cars,
Get more public transport,
Don't just sit in bars,
Use your passport.

Say no to litter,
Don't get new bags,
Seeing it, I feel so bitter,
Don't be grumpy old hags.

So save today, save tomorrow,
You can make a difference,
Don't go and burrow,
So save today and save tomorrow,
You can make a difference.

So save today to
Save tomorrow.

Laura Woodend (11)
Caludon Castle School

Recycle

R ubbish is untidy and very smelly,
E veryone can help by using their recycling bins,
C lothes and shoes can be recycled,
Y oung now but old soon, we can all do our bit!
C ans and bottles can be used again,
L eaves and garden rubbish make great compost,
E nvironmental health helps to make the world free from diseases.

Hannah Kiddie (11)
Caludon Castle School

10

The Large World

The world, the world,
It's a crazy place,
Filled with war,
Yet filled with grace.

People laughing,
People crying,
People living,
People dying.

Smoke filled cities,
Busy towns,
Clean aired countryside,
With cattle all around.

Sandy beaches,
Deep blue sea,
Colourful flowers,
Swaying in the summer breeze.

Lots of countries,
Different time zones,
All under one moon,
In the world, our home.

Nathan Watts (11)
Caludon Castle School

All About Green

The long green grass,
The salty sea water,
The green frog bellows,
As it croaks,
Sitting on its lily pad,
A place it calls its home.

The big green chair,
Is as comfy as a cloud,
Trees decorated in green leaves,
Just like a Christmas tree.

Ryan Packwood (11)
Caludon Castle School

The Big Green, Eco-Friendly, Poetry Machine!

Planet Earth is cool,
So don't be a fool,
Get together a federation,
To save the world's next generation.

Walkin' in your street,
With litter beneath your feet,
Both an eyesore to you,
And others you will meet.

The world is getting hotter,
Because of mankind's greed,
Destroying habitat of polar bear and otter,
Which they really need.

Birds in the sky,
Whales in the sea,
Getting hurt by our pollution,
So what's our solution?

Pollution is vile,
It's not worth your while!

Toni Daniel (11)
Caludon Castle School

Turn It Off!

Turn down that dial,
It is so vile,
To pollute the Earth,
It is worth it
To save Mother Earth.

Take out that plug,
Don't put the rubbish under that lorry,
Turn off that light,
It is so right,
Being green is great.

Nick Ferlisi (12)
Caludon Castle School

Our World

What about the polar bears?
What about the dolphins stuck in the net?
What about the sea turtles in the sea, so deep?
They'll never be as safe as they could be.

Has anyone looked outside lately?
Obviously not, 'cause the world's a state. Yeah.

We need to do something fast,
Otherwise the world will blast,
While we talk, oil takes over the sea,
Please, please do something.

Animals dying while we eat
Their friends and family,
Please stop it now
'Cause I feel like crying.

I wanna help but I can't do it all by myself,
So we need teamwork to save the world.

We can do it!
We can do it!
Yeah!

Carris Bruce (11)
Caludon Castle School

The Deforestation Poem

Think of all them animals,
Their homes slowly being destroyed,
Think of all them monkeys,
Constantly being annoyed.

Hundreds of animals,
With nowhere to go,
So if you hear of
Deforestation, just say . . .
No!

Callum McEneaney (11)
Caludon Castle School

13

Our World Today

Technology risen,
Exercise decreased,
Free health care, less people deceased.

People have grown,
As have our minds,
A variety of race, of all different kinds.

Our lives have lengthened,
And our electric bills,
Now everyone is taking pills.

Guns are all on the streets,
And our litter everywhere,
All the fumes from our cars in the air.

The world is getting hotter,
All from our cars,
Everyone should start walking to their local bars.

People are taking advantage,
Don't take for granted what we have,
Please stop it now.

Bradley Harris (11)
Caludon Castle School

Litter, Litter

Litter, litter everywhere,
Litter, litter here and there,
Litter, litter on my street,
Litter, litter at my feet,
The world's not eco-friendly,
But it needs to be,
Forests are declining,
Plants starting to die,
Animals endangered,
While the human race grows,
We're so selfish,
But no one knows.

Jack William Marsden (11)
Caludon Castle School

14

Green Song

People of the living kingdom,
Stop and listen to my message,
You are wasting our resources now.

Let's look after our planet,
God's the one who began it.

Time to save the inner lands now.

Energy and air pollution,
Drifting in the sky light,
People are using more and more.

Creatures of the living kingdom are
In danger of extinction.

Time to save the inner lands now.

Hope you really understand this,
This ain't funny, this is serious.

Time to save the inner lands now.

Charles Musarurwa (11)
Caludon Castle School

Meltdown

Waters rising over there,
But all of us don't seem to care,
Melting glaciers, animals losing homes,
Extreme weather turning them to bones,
With global warming on its way,
Destroying the planet each and every day,
Our oceans and seas are bound to flood,
Rivers and streams will turn to mud,
So what can we do to save our planet?
Driving cars, maybe we should ban it!
We all just need to do our bit,
Or else our planet's in for it,
It's vital that we play our part,
To give our Earth a brand-new start.

Shannon Power (11)
Caludon Castle School

To Make Earth A Better Place

Litter, litter,
The bins are in no use,
This has to stop,
Don't pollute.

Walk, walk, walk to school,
It can save fossil fuels,
But if the car drives down the hill,
Something will be coming your way called a bill.

War, war,
It can be sore,
Deadly and life risking,
Dangerous and heartbreaking.

Energy, energy,
An important thing in life,
Don't waste it,
It is for everyone, including your wife.

Zak Bremmer (11)
Caludon Castle School

Save The Planet

Did you hear the news this morning?
Energy supplies are falling: don't just sit there snoring!
Go green, keep the place sparkling clean!
The world is being demolished,
It needs some polishing, clean the mess,
Clean the mess and try your best.
Save energy, save this world,
The Earth is heating,
All because of wasting central heating in our homes.

A lack of care, it isn't fair.
Problems of global warming, the Earth is burning.
Do something now and for evermore,
Problems, problems, lurking around.

Heat - melt - and melt equals earthquakes . . .

Amrah Iqbal (11)
Caludon Castle School

Saving The World

We can make the world
A better place,
By putting effort
In every space.

I don't want the world to end,
And nor do you,
So with your help,
We can solve the problem too.

So help me have a solution,
With all this pollution,
It will make the world feel stronger,
And make us live longer.

Let's do it now,
Before it's too late,
So this debate,
Doesn't go on forever.

Danielle Peterson (11)
Caludon Castle School

Donkeys Die Of Sadness

We put all these things into the world,
They make pollution and mess,
All things go into the ozone,
It melts the polar ice caps,
Penguins go down whirlpools,
They get crushed by falls,
They're going extinct,
Rainforests are getting destroyed,
But what about the animals?
Monkeys fall off cliffs of wood,
Iguanas die of pollution,
Donkeys die of sadness,
So look after our world,
As we have not.

Jacob Nilsson (11)
Caludon Castle School

Save Today To Save Tomorrow

Save today to save tomorrow,
Turn the lights off when you go out,
So we don't live in sorrow,
So we won't live in doubt.

Reduce the amount of trees we use,
Reuse the glass too,
Recycle all the paper we use,
So we don't die too.

We're killing our world right now,
Please don't destroy it,
Help us but how?
Instead get fit.

So save today to save tomorrow,
We save the world right now,
Then we win, not live in sorrow,
But how can we save the world?

Emily Jones (11)
Caludon Castle School

Help

Help! Help!
I shout out,
I shout 24/7,
But you don't hear,
I'm dying from pollution!
Carbon dioxide,
And all the rest,
The ozone layer's going frantic,
Winds are getting stronger,
The ice is melting,
So the rain pours in gallons,
But there is hope!
So turn off things you don't need!

Benjhi Dosanjh (11)
Caludon Castle School

Literally

Paper not recycled,
Wrappers not disposed,
All thrown on the floor,
Without a care of the world,
Literally!
Bins not being used,
Recycle bins left to lie on the floor,
Empty bottles not being recycled,
No one cares about the world,
Literally!

Animals dying of unnatural causes,
Helpless mammals becoming extinct,
The world being destroyed,
We are slowly killing the world,
Literally!

So no to litter!

Bethany Watkins (11)
Caludon Castle School

War, Litter And Extinction

Why war? Why do we bother,
To take out guns and kill one another?
When we kill, you are hurting yourself the most,
More than anyone else.

Extinction is awful, animals are dying,
People try to save them but why bother trying?
So just go back and live in your city,
It is your fault elephants are dying of obesity.

Litter is destroying the Earth,
It's dominated since your birth,
So next time you drop litter in the bin,
You will know that you will win.

Luca Hughes (11)
Caludon Castle School

Environment

Recycling is
Important,
Rainforest is
Nature,
Pollution is
The world
And wildlife is
Endangered!

The world is
Collapsing,
And everything's
Running low,
Pollution dying,
And soon that
Could be
You!

Tamara Virdee (12)
Caludon Castle School

Deforestation

Poor little monkeys sitting in a tree,
Dancing and climbing happily,
Monkeys run all in fright,
They can't go any further, life's at an end,
The trees fall and are starting to bend,
Hanging on, not giving up,
All their work has been in vain,
Crash, bang, trees fall and hit the ground,
Monkeys are crushed under the bush,
Covered up, everything's hush,
Other animals see the commotion;
Reptiles; birds; bugs and big cats,
Moving on away from all of that,
Hiding away wishing not to suffer just like that,
Help them now by recycling paper,
And we can save *Mother Nature!*

Gurveer Marva (11)
Caludon Castle School

How The World Goes Around!

The wind sweeps beneath my wings,
Blowing through the trees and plants,
It sets my spirit alight at the second of a blink,
It travels through houses and homes,
Just these little physical changes.

One civil war into a world war,
These few little lives turn into a missing city,
Floods from the rain,
That one tiny grain growing in the grass,
From war to peace.

The sun shines bright down on those rose buds,
Snow falls down upon my nose,
Brown and red leaves pirouette down from crooked branches,
The sky glistens like a clear blue pool,
This is how the world goes around.

Paige Dawson (12)
Caludon Castle School

The Credit Cruncher

We are losing money,
We are going to die,
Because of a monster,
That wears a tie.

And all the young people,
Getting into debt,
They must pay that off,
But they always forget.

What about the younger children,
That will have to survive,
What have we done?
We have destroyed their lives.

Lauren Hancock (11)
Caludon Castle School

Let's Start A Revolution

Let's start a revolution,
To find a solution,
For all this pollution.

We are running out of time,
We need to solve this crime.

In 2050 we might not be here,
And 2050 is very near.

Have some respect for the greenhouse effect,
What do you expect when you smoke your cigarette.

Come on let's start today,
And maybe the future will be OK.

Isabelle Buchanan (11)
Caludon Castle School

War

W et ground, blood-filled massacre,
A nger, hatred, persecution,
R ight or wrong?

I nsults, assaults, bloodbath,
S tupid use of steel and lives.

B itter, sad, lonely, depressing,
A nd dead people, and bereaved families,
D umbest schoolboy in the class of idiotic people, that's war.

N o more weapons,
O r missiles, or bombs,
W ar must be stopped, to save the world.

Thomas Killestein (11)
Caludon Castle School

Why?

Why? Why? Why?
I say it again and again,
They know I'm dying,
So when will it end?

They poison me, they hurt me,
But all I want to know is why?

My ice caps are melting,
Animals are going to die,
So all I need to know is why?

If you kill me, then you're killing everyone else,
Why are you doing this to yourself?

Laura Kelsey (11)
Caludon Castle School

Save Coventry

Do you have a solution
To stop pollution,
It is about the trees,
Or the bumblebees?

Don't use the car,
You can cycle far,
If you drop litter,
You will feel bitter.

If you smoke, you will choke,
So stop making pollution,
You can make a difference.

John Hazikyriakos-Fry & Jacob Reid (11)
Caludon Castle School

Water

W hen you next chuck something in the pond, watch the water
   Turn green and think about what you are doing.

A nd when you next do something stupid, just think to
   Yourself what you are doing 'cause you are mad when you
   Pollute 'cause you're bad if you pollute.

T o your mum and your dad, you seem all good,
   But if they knew you'd pollute, they would stop and shout.

E ven though you are normally good, you have no excuses,
   Because you wreck it and pollute.

R eceive the punishment and deal with it.

Zachary Thomas (11)
Caludon Castle School

Help The Wildlife

Help the wildlife, it's in danger,
There's a stranger that chops the trees down
To your knees, so can you do a favour please?
If you burn the trees, the animals' lives will be in danger,
Where will they sleep?
Where will they eat?
How will they live?
So come on and give some help,
Will you please?

Charlie Bennett (11)
Caludon Castle School

War

W ar is a very big battle,
A ll the powerful people competing for our country,
R eels of shields are used all day, are you confused?

Jessica Fretwell (12)
Caludon Castle School

24

Homelessness

Being homeless is a bad thing,
It's like a really bad sting,
Children are sad, and their parents are too,
But they don't know who is going to help them,
They don't know who.
Sitting on the streets, sad and cold,
And the small babies have no one to hold,
So please, help homeless people, do,
You never know, one day, it could be you.

Jenny Louis (11)
Caludon Castle School

Pollution

P iles of litter,
O zone layer destroying,
L ots of dangerous gases,
L ater destruction of the year,
U nder rocks the animals hide,
T he world is getting hotter,
I gloos melting,
O ur atmosphere is being destroyed,
N ow it's time to change our ways.

Ross Bowell (11)
Caludon Castle School

Recycle

R epresents the eco team,
E ven if you don't have experience,
C all for help if you don't understand,
Y our world will be a better place,
C aring for your environment,
L eaves a cleaner area,
E ven making you much cleaner.

Mansi Gohil (12)
Caludon Castle School

Save The Country, Save The World!

The oil is building up,
Pollution is closing in,
The Earth is being destroyed!
We must stop pollution, or else.
We have too much oil,
We must produce less,
If we don't, the Earth will dry up!
Just imagine, no water at all.

Joshua Dennis (11)
Caludon Castle School

Being Green

Being green,
Keeps us clean,
Recycle paper,
It will help you later,
Walk to school,
Then you'll be cool,
Don't use the car,
It won't get you far.

Amir Ahmed (11)
Caludon Castle School

Global Warming

Global warming, global warming,
It is coming soon,
Global warming, global warming,
I hope it doesn't stay,
The polar bear, the polar bear,
Doesn't have time to spare,
Because of the sun, it might lose its hair,
The ice, the ice is melting quickly,
It will all be gone by 2050!

Deborah Smith (11)
Hillcrest School

The Panic Room

As I entered this panicked room,
Faces all buffed and red-nosed,
All their eyes wide open, but the same all closed,
Big gasps and smiles, all round, but fake,
For I who entered the room.

But my entrance of this room,
Was not my like, I was baffled,
Scattering on the floor nearby all raffled,
My smile, was wiped off and quickly turned into a frown,
Not like what I had in mind,
When I entered the room.

Before my entrance took place,
Was it the same as it were now?
Was what I know as disgrace,
A happy pleasant face?
But all has changed,
Since I entered that room.

Something strange about this room,
Big, incredible, but no thought,
No ambitions, nought,
I feared that these people's perspective
On life was abandoned,
Wishing my entrance did not take place,
Not in this panic room.

But what has this panic room become?
A mess? A long term decision?
These people's eyes open, but the same all closed,
But do they know how much their ignorance showed,
This shocking fact all unravelled like the ones on the floor,
That panicked me,
That panic room.

Morgan James (13)
Hillcrest School

Our Small World

The world is finite,
Resources are scarce.

Coal is burnt
And gas exploded.

Wells are dry
And air polluted.

Oil is going,
Ores depleted.

Land is sinking,
Seas are rising.

Fires will rage,
With Man to fan it.

Things are bad
And will be worse.

Forests out
And soil eroded.

Dust is blowing,
Trees are uprooted.

Drains receive,
What is excreted.

Man is far too *enterprising!*

Soon we'll have a plundered planet.

Karman Chan (14)
Hillcrest School

As The Dawn Breaks

I hear the songs of the twittering birds,
But all of a sudden, the sweet sounds
Are drowned by the noise of the engines at rush hour,
Carbon monoxide is all around us,
Try and ditch your car and use the bus.

Tanzeela Hussain (11)
Hillcrest School

Animals Down In Numbers

Now here's a thing,
Animal extinction is happening,
What do we do?
I know, how about you?

Out there on the ice,
There's an animal, soft and nice,
Polar bear is its name,
And they're dying such a shame.

They are killed for their furs,
How often this occurs,
Always on the news,
Another life to lose.

Slaughtered by Man,
Since transport began,
Protect them now,
Others say 'How?'

Think about those poor things,
Even them with wings,
Dodo birds were once here,
Since 1681 that year.

Could it be global warming
Or the world forming?
What do we do?
I know, how about you?

Emma Finney (12)
Hillcrest School

Litter

L itter in the park and
I n the streets,
T he rubbish, the world, not neat,
T he children want to play,
E ven when there is litter,
R ight now they can because we have recycled.

Samantha Daniels (11)
Hillcrest School

Rainforest

Juicy fruit growing on the beautiful trees,
Nice and fresh for the animals to eat,
Smell the fragrance surrounded around you,
Oranges, apples, pears and grapes.

Cheeky birds chirping silently in the trees,
Robins fluttering their wings with a little red breast,
Birds chirping silently in their canopies,
Listen, shhh, just listen,
Monkeys swinging tree to tree.

Relax back, sit comfortable, listen,
Oh no! There's nothing left behind,
Not even an animal.

Pollution that's what, oil spillage,
Like not enough people cared.

Too much electricity,
Too much gas,
Too much pollution,
To explore and drill for oil.

No more monkeys,
No more birds,
No more robins,
No more trees,
No more fruit!

Samera Kauser (12)
Hillcrest School

Litter

The litter outside makes me sick,
The litter outside makes me wanna shake to my knees.

The litter outside makes the area look dirty,
The litter outside makes me wanna scream out for mercy.

The litter on the street makes it unwalkable,
The litter on the street makes the area look terrible.

Sarafina Farrell (15)
Hillcrest School

When You Look Into My Eyes

When you look into my eyes, what do you see?
My fur,
My meat,
My affection,
My happiness.
When you look into my eyes, what do you see?
My blood,
My heart,
My friendliness,
My smile.
When you look into my eyes, what do you see?
Yourself,
Your thoughts,
My potential,
My hope.
When you look into my eyes, what do you see?
Emptiness,
Unworthiness,
My complexity,
My prowess.
When you look into my eyes, what do you see?
My fear,
My death,
My dreams,
My life.

Katharine June Parker (13)
Hillcrest School

The Tiger

Roar goes the tiger,
As I pass him in the zoo,
When I was going to the loo.

I notice that he looks like a fire,
Because he is orange,
The black stripes on his fur are the twigs
In the fire.

Lisa Jones (12)
Hillcrest School

No Matter!

Walking down the street,
No shoes,
Bare feet,
Knocking on every door,
No vacancy,
Too poor,
Starts to rain,
No umbrella,
Such pain,
'Look at that black man!'
They shout,
No doubt,
No matter!
Even though I walk through the street,
Bare feet,
I feel grass in my toes,
No matter!
Rain's no pain,
Just nature,
No matter!
Let them call me what they want,
I have all I need,
A sunflower seed,
Which will grow, grow, grow,
Until . . .

Saboorah Rana (11)
Hillcrest School

Nature

N is for numerous disasters,
A is for atmosphere, letting us breathe,
T is for trees, swaying in the wind,
U is for universe, where we all live,
R is for recycling, papers and bottles,
E is for environment, which we need to protect.

Kirsty Elliker (11)
Hillcrest School

32

Black Or White?

Black or white?
We all fly the same kite,
Even though it seems,
You're the odd one out,
Well you're not, without a doubt!

Remember that we are all the same,
Even with different names!
Black as the night,
White as the snow,
Let it in,
But don't let it go.

No one's the same,
It may be a pain,
When you look different,
But what can we do?
When we are blessed like this,
If your name's Molly or your name's Chris.

Don't feel down,
If someone turns your smile into a frown,
Just think,
Black or white!
We're all the same!

Madiyah Hussain (11)
Hillcrest School

Save Our World

Cold winds blow,
Oil pours,
Fish dead,
Driving my car,
Trees choke,
The noise bangs,
In my head,
The scream of
The rainforest.

Connie Hackley (11)
Hillcrest School

Disappearing Quickly

When I look outside my window,
I do not see the green grass and the
Early morning sun rising anymore,
I see buildings,
Blocking out my view,
I do not see the green grass,
Through the looking glass,
I see car fumes,
Building up and up,
Grey fog,
I do not see the badgers on the green,
I see rats,
Scurrying through, coming from the rubbish,
That we drop, I couldn't see this coming,
The beauty of nature is disappearing,
Slowly it's going,
But I ask myself,
Who are the ones destroying it?
Who?
Those beautiful views have gone . . .
Disappearing quicker and quicker,
Right in front of my eyes . . .

Joanna Bashford (14)
Hillcrest School

Black Or White?

Black or white,
What's the difference?
They're all the same to me,
You could be pink,
Purple, red or periwinkle,
Still doesn't matter to me.

You shouldn't care,
Who they say you are,
As long as you,
Know who you are.

Esterina Kegi (11)
Hillcrest School

Stay Green

If you want life green then you better keep it clean
And recycle that old machine.

Don't drop rubbish on the floor,
This is a big *no-no!*
So stop the show!

Get into the beat and tap your feet
And say we've got to clean up this heap.

You'll make our planet a heck of a lot better,
If you just listen to this letter
And apply it which would be even better.

I've got to go now so follow my rules
And I'll show you how!
Always be clean and not so mean . . .
Else goodbye to the future . . .
Are you pleased?

Now all I've got to say is
Stay very, very *green!*

Samoya Cowan (11)
Hillcrest School

Pollution Everywhere

Pollution, pollution,
Pollution everywhere,
Pollution in the ocean,
Pollution in the air,
Please stop pollution,
It's not a good thing to do,
It's not good for animals,
It's not good for me and you,
It's not a happy thing to do,
Cars cause pollution,
Even me and you,
Please stop pollution,
It's a bad thing to do!

Melissa Stowe (12)
Hillcrest School

Pollution

Flowers flowing in the breeze,
Lots of them around for bees.

Fish are swimming in the seas,
Also swimming around my knees.

People going past in boats,
Standing there in their coats.

Getting off to get in a car,
Driving off to somewhere far.

Children crying about pollution,
They don't know about a solution.

Flowers dying in the breeze,
None of them around for bees.

No fish are swimming in the seas,
Dirt is all around my knees.

A tear is falling from my face,
Wishing to live in a better place.

Toni Phillips-Lewis (13)
Hillcrest School

Don't Drop Me!

If I don't pick up that bit of litter,
It could float into the sea,
If it floats into the sea,
A whale could swallow it whole,
If a whale swallows it whole,
It could get stuck in his blowhole,
If it got stuck in his blowhole,
It could have breathing problems,
If it has breathing problems, it might die,
If it dies, it could be a female,
If it is a female, it won't be able to reproduce,
If it doesn't reproduce, whales could become extinct,
I should definitely pick up that bit of litter.

Hope Fields (11)
Hillcrest School

36

Leaves, Leaves Everywhere

When the autumn leaves,
Blow past in a breeze,
It makes me shiver,
It makes me quiver.

Quiver like a leaf,
Children play mischief,
How it changes their behaviour,
Even the narrator,
Which is me,
Standing under a leafless tree,
I am so cold,
Traditional stories are being told,
All of the flowers withered away,
'That's ought to happen,' some people say,
Here I am,
Standing near a tram,
Getting swirled away,
What a wonderful, autumn's day!

Sonal Patel (12)
Hillcrest School

Trees And Flowers

Trees and flowers grow everywhere,
Just like us humans can be anywhere,
Without plants, it will be hard to breathe,
Make me just want to heave,
We wouldn't live,
With no water, air, plants,
As I live with oxygen,
It's like a world full of fun,
Stop pollution coming around you and me,
Make the air all clear so I can see,
Save the world from coming apart,
From a dangerous gas just like a Jurassic fart,
All together the world will be full of love,
Peace and friendship.

Michelle Cheung (11)
Hillcrest School

Black, Brown Or White, Why Do We Care?

Black, brown or white, why do we care?
Why does it matter if we're dark or we're fair?
It still matters what colour we are,
The dream, civil rights, we've not moved on that far.

Why am I hated because of the tone of my skin?
Is this the equal society we claim we're living in?
Why can't we see that we're all the same,
That feeding the hate just causes us pain.

Being black is my reality,
I'm not judged on my personality,
I'm not admired for the way I was raised,
But feared for what the media portrays.

Feared for the evil a few commit,
Even though all nations are committing it,
So black, brown or white, why do we care?
We fear what is different, we need to stop fear.

Sheneel Miesha Rodway (13)
Hillcrest School

Life In The Pond

Racoons scurry, hunting for food,
Frogs hop and pop and peep,
Snapping turtles hide under their shells,
Deer prance all over the grass,
Loons waddle and swim,
Salamanders crawl under rocks,
Otters slide down the riverbanks,
Great blue herons snap fish in their mouth,
Moose hide behind bushes,
Swans dunk their heads in deep water,
Dragonflies fly high and low,
Ducks waddle near the pond,
Sunfish lay eggs in the water,
Beavers slap their tails on the water,
The pond is bursting with life.

Sophie Overgaard (13)
Hillcrest School

The Love Of Nature!

Nature, nature pure,
Nature, how I love nature,
Nature, where will I be without you?
Nature, nature where will I be?
The green leaves that surround me.

Nature, don't worry I will save you,
No one can break you down,
No, not on my watch,
So tell me how can the wind breeze through you.

I'm your friend, so what do you say?
The trees and beautiful flowers, even the wind,
How I love nature,
That's my middle name, nature is my thing,
So cheer up and let's dance with the wind.

I love nature.

Mildred Mukwende (11)
Hillcrest School

All Year Round

Trees, trees, trees,
Leaves, leaves, leaves,
From green to red,
From red to brown,
They change their colour all year round,
The sun beating down,
On the grass all around,
The lake is glistening,
The birds are tweeting,
The sun goes down,
The snow begins to fall,
No longer hear their call,
The lake becomes still,
No movement at all,
Just the trees left,
Standing proud and tall.

Gemma Oldsworth (14)
Hillcrest School

Being Homeless

Here I am all alone,
Here I am all alone,
It's cold and dark,
The foxes are out,
Here I am all alone.

I'm cold and hungry,
My clothes are torn,
My shoes are too small,
I don't know what to do,
I wish I had a home.

Here I am all alone,
Here I am all alone,
I can see someone coming,
Maybe I'll get some food,
Here I am all alone.

Rebecca Jones (13)
Hillcrest School

Green Is The Issue

G reen is the two of our issues,
   Our answer to solve is to destroy you.
R emember the days when all was well,
   The air was clean and the world was swell.
E missions, ignitions all have symptoms showing,
   The dying world we happen to live in.
E ngage, interact not long is the fact,
   Because when it's gone, there's no bringing it back.
N ever again will we have this world,
   Because when we're gone, there's no boy and no girl.

Green is the two of our issues,
To solve or destroy, which one will you choose?
One is the problem, two is the unknown,
But I'll give you a clue,
An answer is needed and the rest is up to you . . .

Yusra Hussein (14)
Hillcrest School

Environmental Poem

E is for the energy we waste,
N is for the never-ending suffering,
V is for the volume of water rising,
I is for the ice caps that melt,
R is for the rain that always comes,
O is for the ozone layer that is being destroyed,
N is for the normal happenings changing,
M is for the meaningless deaths,
E is for the edge of truth about the world,
N is for the numerous occasions when the world goes wrong,
T is for the terrible harm on the environment.

P is for the polar bears that are dying,
O is for the ocean levels rising rapidly,
E is for the Earth dying slowly,
M is for the many things we *should* do to help!

Sybella Buttress (14)
Hillcrest School

Reduce ... Reuse ... Recycle ...

Recycle .. Recycle ... recycle ...

Throwing garbage, making a mountain,
Doesn't help being a friendly environment.

Making the environment clean and spotless,
Will help everyone live in a clean place.

Recycling cans,
Recycling paper,
Will help everyone to do the same.

Throwing things, throwing gum,
Makes a bad environment.

Use things which can be
Reduced ... reused ...
Recycled ...

Aleena Akhtar (14)
Hillcrest School

The World

What is going on? What do I see?
Is this a dream or is it reality?
War is unhealthy to the human race and
All we want to do is make the world a better place.
Climate change is around, the ice is melting down,
But no one is going to help, not even Gordon Brown.
People now complain whether your skin is black or white
And all the teenagers want to do is put up a nasty fight,
Poverty on the rise, not only affecting the Third World,
But litter on the streets, infested with worms,
With a hole in the ozone layer and the world falling apart,
Will there ever be a glorious start?

So all I can say, is stop your disastrous ways,
Go with the flow and take life slow.

Humarya Jubeen (13)
Hillcrest School

Notice Me As I Am

You're blinded by our differences,
My culture makes no sense to you,
Yet I'm the persecuted one,
And you're the red, white and blue,
Of human ignorance, I am in despair,
The comments I receive,
About my skin colour,
Or why I don't show my hair,
Why do you deprive me of what I deserve,
Is the colour of your community all you preserve?
Martin Luther said, 'I have a dream!'
But not yet has it been seen,
So why not unite everyone together?
Then live in peace forever and ever.

Hafsa Duale (13)
Hillcrest School

Nature

Nature is beautiful,
Nature is fun,
Nature is like Marmite,
You either love it or hate it.

Nature is blue,
Nature is green,
Nature is every colour,
Possibly seen.

Nature is true,
Nature is you,
Nature is me,
Nature will forever be free.

Simran Kaur Chahal (11)
Hillcrest School

Furry Cats

Cats are soft,
Cats are furry,
Cats are cute and sweet.

They love to run,
They love to play,
When they are hungry,
They eat and drink,
Until they fall asleep.

But most cats are abandoned,
Left on the streets,
They wait and wait,
Until they are rescued.

Deanna Deakin (12)
Hillcrest School

Save The World, It Matters

Litter is all on the floor,
Every winter's day,
Why don't we pick it up,
We are drowning in a way.

It's up to our feet,
It's up to our nose,
It's coming to our shoulders,
It's suffocating our toes.

Use your tin cans,
As telephones,
We won't be bothered,
But she shops may moan.

Chelsea Sacha Stagg (11)
Hillcrest School

Appreciate All

Black, white, Asian or mixed race,
We all have different coloured faces,
We are different cultures
And we live different lifestyles.

So why should we be treated like we're dirt,
Mixed up in a posh, clean area?
We should appreciate that we are different from one another,
Can you imagine everyone the same?
The same colour,
Same hair,
Same eyes,
Now, wouldn't that give you a bit of a scare?

Zara Hamid (12)
Hillcrest School

Everything Green

Grass is green,
We are mean,
We cut it endlessly.

Trees help us have energy,
We cut them down,
We have shorter lives.

We must be eco-friendly,
To help our environment.

Pollution is bad,
It kills us quicker,
Save the ozone layer.

Toral Jutha (11)
Hillcrest School

Homeless

I live on the streets,
Because I am homeless,
It is cold, scary and dangerous.

I have only the clothes that I am wearing,
People pass with a strange look,
I think to myself, *why do they keep staring?*

I miss my family,
All because of the terrible war,
Sometimes I hear that sound,
That bombed my house,
That roar.

Mariam Jan (12)
Hillcrest School

In Any Other World . . .

In any other world,
You could smile and mean it,
You could see pure running water and feel fresh,
You could see new flowers growing and feel happy,
You could take a deep breath and smell fresh air not the smoke,
You could look out of the window and see beautiful green parks,
You could walk outside and see clean streets with no litter,
Do you want this?

Well, say goodbye to this perfect world and
Return to the slowly ruined world we live in!

Why kill it? Do something about it!

Serina Patel (15)
Hillcrest School

Mother Earth

Global warming isn't hard to explain,
It leaves Mother Earth crying with pain,
This hurts our planet in every single way
And air pollution can carry on for days,
If we don't do something,
We will end up with nothing,
The animals living in the wildlife will not longer be alive,
There are solutions to these issues,
So don't just throw them away in tissues!
Make the world a safer, cleaner and a
Beautiful place for us to live in.

Abeera Ali (11)
Hillcrest School

The Colour That We Are

Is it the colour black that you hate?
The colour that you wear,
The words that you say,
That make people drop a tear?
We're just a colour, darker than the rest,
With the same sense - perhaps better than the best,
Don't forget, TV was once black and white,
But colour's what makes the world so bright,
Does it matter what colour we are?
We're just darker than the rest,
Perhaps better than the best.

Chevanique Thomas (12)
Hillcrest School

Nature

Nature, nature pure and green,
It's so beautiful to be seen,
Keep it good, keep it clean,
Everything in good condition, nice and sheen,
All beautiful to us but we don't help,
But if we don't act, it will melt,
Pollute our air and ruin our flowers,
Running electricity for our towers,
Don't ruin our houses and our lives,
Think about the young, think about nature's young,
We're ruining the land, we're ruining our existence!

Sian Mills (11)
Hillcrest School

Rainforest

Why are people cutting down trees?
Don't they understand that we need to breathe?
Low oxygen levels we are going to face,
Why don't we stop and make the world a better place.

It's not fair that we have to suffer so,
Because in a few years time, oxygen levels will be low,
So stop it now, before it's too late
And help the world become a better place!

Please help us do what is right,
Otherwise we will be battling a lonely fight.

Rebecca Walkley (13)
Hillcrest School

Family

Mom, Dad,
Brother and sister,
Gone, gone far away,
Never seen them for a long way.

Every family member counts,
No matter how they are,
Grumpy, mean, ugly, pretty,
Nice, horrible.

Just look after your family,
They're the closest thing.

Abigail Elizabeth Green (11)
Hillcrest School

Keep Dolphins Safe!

Dolphins are beautiful, friendly and gentle,
Most people who litter the sea are sometimes a bit naughty and mental,
In the land and sea, there is so much pollution,
So let us think of a healthy solution:
Keep your rubbish in the bins,
So you don't hurt their delicate fins,
Don't end the water world just the matter of waste,
It could kill the dolphins as they are able to taste,
Never litter and let the outstanding dolphins shine and glitter.

Kiran Singh Sole (11)
Hillcrest School

War Is Me

War is sad,
Like my feelings,
People don't like who others are,
Like my life,
No one likes me for who I am,
One country does not like another for who they are,
It's all the truth,
And one day we just have to face the truth,
War is me,
I am war . . .

Jessica Cohen (13)
Hillcrest School

Trees, Trees, Trees

Trees, trees, trees,
They give us paper, oxygen plus air,
We breathe air because they care!
So please, please, please,
Don't cut down our glorious trees!

Dannielle Morris (11)
Hillcrest School

Pollution

Pollution, pollution everywhere,
If you want it to stop,
Just turn off your engine and breathe in the air,
Ride a bike or walk the dog,
Leave the car keys at home and go for a jog.

So breathe in easy without having to worry
About pollution and when the trees are falling down
It's partly your fault,
So when your world's being destroyed, it's all your fault.

Sarah Johnson (12)
Hillcrest School

You And Me, Him And Her

You and me, him and her can make the world a better place,
None of us will have to live in such a disgrace.
You and me, him and her need to tell people to pick up their junk,
If they don't, then our world will become a bigger and bigger dump.

You and me, him and her need to recycle to save the Earth,
They get made into things to help us buy things
For what our money is worth,
You and me, him and her are all a part of this world,
Remember all that I have wrote and make sure it is learnt.

Leshea Blake (13)
Hillcrest School

Beautiful World

The world is as beautiful as a flower,
The ocean flows from side to side,
The wind whistles through the trees,
Don't change or destroy the world,
Keep it the way it is.

Maryama Dhahir (11)
Hillcrest School

With Nature

Gardens are green and full of nature,
With the animals greatest atmosphere,
With falling down trees and oxygen dying.

Gardens are green and full of nature,
With the mountains erupting our grass is frying.

Gardens are green and full of nature,
With our paper not recycling our world is wasting away.

Gardens are green and full of nature.

Chadene Skerritt (12)
Hillcrest School

Watta 'Bout The Animals?

Climate change, CO_2,
All of this is bad for you!
Chopping trees,
Missing bees,
You're killing the world, so stop it please!
Think of all the bunnies
And what about that fox?
They're gonna be cold in winter
And you can't provide them socks!

Johanna Liang (11)
Hillcrest School

Poverty

People are starving, people are dying,
Others say they didn't know, but we know they're lying,
Will you help them? They need it desperately,
Because right now, they're in poverty!

Lamees Al-Qahtani (13)
Hillcrest School

Sad Side Of Nature

Standing on a hill, on the grass,
Looking at these cars going past.

Everything is changing since the world's bad time,
I stand here on hillside, writing this sad, sad rhyme.

The birds now fly so low in the sky,
The world is changing, 'Why oh why?'

People are sitting here watching death come by.

Sarah Eltaher (14)
Hillcrest School

Extinction!

Animals get killed every day
And extinction isn't very far away,
Sooner or later, they're all going to die
And we couldn't say anything because we were too shy,
Tigers and bears all the same,
We hang our heads in God's shame,
We need to stop the poachers right here, right now,
Or else they will kill the last baby cow.

Olivia Kelsey (12)
Hillcrest School

Britain The Dump

Packet's here, boxes there,
Lots of rubbish everywhere,
Paper and cardboard sitting in the bins,
When these items can be recycled things,
Cigarette droppings in corners, on paths,
Cigarette ashes wiped into a stash,
Why is Britain such a mess?
Me and you could make it less.

Danielle Brown-Grizzle (13)
Hillcrest School

Our Environment!

I look at the world
And all the pollution,
I ask myself,
What's the solution?

When I look out the window,
I see litter and fights,
Something needs to be done,
Day and night,

I go outside,
Rubbish I smell,
Litter everywhere,
It looks like a spell.

When I want to have fun,
I see people with tears,
Where will this end
And take our fears?
So what are you waiting for?
Go and save the world. *Now!*

Fahima Ali (11)
Hodge Hill Sports & Enterprise College

Our World

Our world, our world,
The greatest place is our world,
In and out to the shops we go,
Happy and merry, not a place to show,
The lovely weather but now not better,
But ruined by our pollution,
Weather help to stop the world from falling,
To tear apart our homes and families,
Our world, our world, the greatest place is our world,
To help our wonderful, big, green world,
Stop chopping rainforests to a great bundle,
Climate change, poverty, war and litter,
Help the world!

Annam Javid Sabbah (12)
Hodge Hill Sports & Enterprise College

53

Healing The Earth!

Switch things off like electricity,
You may just cough or may be poorly.

The Earth is sick, sick, sick,
She may be, get a cross or a tick.

Must recycle paper, paper, paper,
There might be stranger danger, danger.

The Earth has pollution, pollution, pollution,
So let's find a solution, solution, solution.

Stop cutting trees, trees, trees,
But dogs have fleas, fleas, fleas.

There shouldn't be cars, cars, cars,
They should be on Mars, Mars, Mars.

Use a bus or bike, bike, bike,
Or maybe camp or hike, hike, hike.

Stop using factories, factories, factories,
And start using batteries, batteries, batteries!

Umer Hussain (12)
Hodge Hill Sports & Enterprise College

Poverty

I go to school,
Five years later, I go to work,
I feed my kids,
I have a car to ride in.

But I still believe that I'm not better than people,
But what I don't realise is there are people much
Worse off than me who have no life.

I spend and spend on myself,
Not knowing people are crying out there,
Crying for help.

Five years later, I'm now begging for money,
And no one is helping me.

Nouha Rakeeb (13)
Hodge Hill Sports & Enterprise College

Our Home

There is a place in you that you love,
It could be the Earth,
The Earth is dying,
People are crying,
If you try, you can save it,
The Earth is in your soul,
Not in your heart,
Let's save the Earth.

Make the Earth a better place,
Me, you and the human race,
People are destroying the Earth,
There's bombing, graffiti, littering,
Destroying the place,
The Earth is our home.

Let's save our home,
Let's save our Earth,
Make it a better place,
For us and the human race.

Sohail Javed (13)
Hodge Hill Sports & Enterprise College

Now It May Seem . . .

Now it may seem a little hard to do,
But a little of it can make the biggest difference,
Are you listening?
Are you reading?
Show some,
Spread some,
Get together and make some,
I'm sure you've heard about it,
Felt it,
Maybe even read about it,
Why not spread it,
The world,
A little can change it.

Nazesh Al-Nisa (15)
Hodge Hill Sports & Enterprise College

Life Is Short!

People going . . .
People dying . . .
People leaving this world . . .
All because of war!
People fight and fight
And carry on fighting,
Killing people!
Bombings, terrorists!
Why do these people like to kill
Innocent people?
Who have families,
Children,
And
Their
Whole
Life
Ahead of
Them!

Sabah Nisa (13)
Hodge Hill Sports & Enterprise College

Senses Of Mother Nature

I can see the polluted rivers,
When I look, I really shiver.

I can taste the acid rain,
On my tongue again and again.

I can hear the trees yelling,
Oh please, oh please stop cutting.

I can smell the dirty litter,
Why couldn't you litter glitter?

I can feel the weather changing,
This is due to global warming.

My sixth sense is my fear,
But I never ever shed a tear.

Abdiaziz Ali (13)
Hodge Hill Sports & Enterprise College

56

Save The World!

When you see the world,
Litter, oil and pollution,
You think to yourself,
What's the solution?

All the oil from boats,
Killing animals,
To make fur coats,
Is this right?

The answer is no!
People must stop and save the world,
If people don't do this,
There will be no world!

Swearing, violence and fights,
Can end up very dreadful,
People are very sorry,
Offenders are regretful.

Harry Atkins (11)
Hodge Hill Sports & Enterprise College

Precious Earth

Earth is the most precious,
Thing in the universe,
There is only one and
There will be nothing else like it.

When there is light, it shines so bright,
So why do we fight?
What about the bleeding Earth?
We humans have destroyed everything
And know why we cannot even sing?

We just sing for fame,
It's not a game,
If you want to save the Earth,
Stop polluting our Earth and
Stop shedding blood.

Ash Nawaz (13)
Hodge Hill Sports & Enterprise College

Beautiful

Earth is a beautiful place to live,
And let's make it a better place,
And this is a place that could be much better
And brighter than tomorrow,
And let's try to keep the Earth clean because of food and disease,
And the Earth is round like a ball,
And it makes me feel whole,
The world is feeling good,
Don't let us destroy it,
And let us try to keep surroundings clean,
Because of the Earth,
And let us work hard to make it a more beautiful place,
The air and trees are oxygen,
Let's keep it because of breathing and
Let us keep the water for the Earth,
And make it a good drink for the world
And let's make our life better for tomorrow.

Ajibode Michael (16)
Hodge Hill Sports & Enterprise College

Untitled

Ice caps melting,
Polar bears dying,
As their homes are
Being destroyed
Because
Of us.

Soft snow is melting,
Penguins decreasing,
Because
Of us.

Keep recycling,
Never stop
And stop
Using too much gas.

Ehtasham Ahmed (11)
Hodge Hill Sports & Enterprise College

Living On A Space Station

Picking up litter is not a crime,
But if you drop it you could end up with a fine,
I would love to look outside and see nice fresh, healthy grass,
So imagine what you could do with a 30-pupiled class,
Recycling household items is fun and cool,
In every family, it should be a number one rule.

From composting food to recycling paper,
We should all do it now, rather than later,
When leaving the room, switch off appliances and lights,
Saving energy for those cold, winter nights,
It would be much healthier walking or riding to school,
To save carbon emissions and cut down on fuel,
Taking holidays in England and The British Isles,
Cuts down on carbon footprints and reduces air miles.

Preserving the planet for the future generation,
Even though they might be living on a space station.

Janessa Prescod (12)
Hodge Hill Sports & Enterprise College

A Calling For Help!

Trees are going,
Grass is going,
Sooner or later,
The Earth will be going.

Animals are dying,
Plants are dying,
The way things are going,
The Earth will be dying.

Pollution is killing the Earth,
People are killing the Earth,
If people recycled,
If the world recycled,
Sooner or later,
The Earth will be recycled.

Mason Scott McDermott (13)
Hodge Hill Sports & Enterprise College

The World

You give me honey,
I give you money,
Will there be a time,
When there is no crime?
When there is war,
You are no more,
If there is no sky,
There will be no flies,
When there are mice,
There is nothing nice,
There are people dying,
Your mum is crying,
It is too long,
To end the song.

Qamar Hussain (15)
Hodge Hill Sports & Enterprise College

Go Green

This is our planet, go green,
Then I realised it wasn't clean,
We all use fuels,
And waste oil,
We have been spoilt,
100 years ago, we didn't have cars,
No electricity,
This is the cost to keep Earth healthy,
So everyone go green,
And keep our planet clean,
There are problems in the world,
That one man can't fix,
We all need to mix
And go green.

Azim Yousuf (12)
Hodge Hill Sports & Enterprise College

60

The Crying Earth

Seeing the world cry is such a painful sight,
Anywhere you go children are living in pain with nothing,
Very little trees are standing, can you hear them waiting?
Every river being polluted by us,
What has the world done to deserve us?
The world is being stamped on and being killed just because of us,
Help the children in poverty,
Save them you must,
Every time you look outside, the world being hurt by careless people,
Every single piece of rubbish you throw, you are killing the world,
Anymore damage, the Earth will no longer be here,
Rather than the Earth being killed, you should help,
There is no love or happiness around us anymore,
Heal the world before it's too late.

Sana Hussain (13)
Hodge Hill Sports & Enterprise College

Help Save The World

Switch off your lights,
When you don't need them,
So this world would
Be a better place for you and the human race.

Reduce your carbon footprint,
By not using your car,
Why not catch the bus,
So this world would be a better place,
For you and the entire human race.

If we try to stop global warming,
By not leaving the TV on,
Make the Earth a better place,
For you and the human race.

Yussuf Omar (13)
Hodge Hill Sports & Enterprise College

There's A Place In The World

There's a place in the world,
Where there's harmony,
We can protect it with a shield,
If we don't pollute,
Then there will be less global warming,
And less storms and more sun,
Then the world would be more fun,
The snow would be a brighter white
And then the world would be a better sight,
There's a place in the world,
Where all the seasons can dance
And the world will be less cold,
Then maybe we will get one more chance.

Sampson Baillie (13)
Hodge Hill Sports & Enterprise College

Saving The World

Stop all the drugs,
Save the world,
Stop all the killing,
Save the world,
Stop all the killing,
Save the world,
Stop racism,
Save the world,
Stop war,
Save the world,
Stop the pollution,
Save the world,
No more crime and hate.

Ayola Hall (13)
Hodge Hill Sports & Enterprise College

Pollution

Pollution is a terrible thing,
Stop it to be a king,
Stop throwing litter on the floor,
A lot less mess, that's for sure.

Our country is so mean,
It never does even clean,
There's bags and food on the floor,
People keep doing it even more.

Listen to this poem,
Understand the meaning,
Then you get the feeling,
Of a good thing.

Rayhaan Khan (12)
Hodge Hill Sports & Enterprise College

Save The World

Stop the pollution,
By saving electricity,
Stop the pollution,
You'll save your city.

Recycle, recycle,
Don't throw stuff away,
Recycle, recycle,
You'll save the trees by the way.

Litter, litter,
Don't throw it on the floor,
Litter, litter,
You'll save even more!

Junaid Mohammed (11)
Hodge Hill Sports & Enterprise College

The World's Going Nowhere

Driving cars causes pollution,
Giving us a difficult solution,
It destroys the world, animals and nature,
Hurting every little creature.

Littering the floors,
Not caring anymore,
Not looking around,
Completely out of your bounds.

The world is a mess,
Because of your stupidness,
Bring this to an end,
Make the world your friend!

Aimen Akkil (13)
Hodge Hill Sports & Enterprise College

Save The World

S ave the animals,
A ir needs to be back,
V ery little trees are left,
E arth is dying and it needs to be back.

T here are people dying,
H eal the world's wounds,
E arth will be gone, if you don't care.

W here has the sun gone?
O ur world is going,
R ather you save the world than sit,
L ove needs to be back,
D o it for the safety so the people can be back.

Anisa Parveen (13)
Hodge Hill Sports & Enterprise College

What Would Make The World A Better Place?

To make the world a better place,
We need to recycle all over the place,
From recycling our cans, glass paper and plastic,
To turning off plugs and lights that's great and fantastic,
Fill the kettle, only halfway full,
Use the shower not a bath,
Use less water and keep our dams full,
We all need to do our little bit,
Otherwise we'll end up living in a pit,
Recycling stuff is really good,
If you're not trying, you'll live rough!

Emma Groom (12)
Hodge Hill Sports & Enterprise College

Pollution

Pollution is a terrible thing,
Pollution can make the world shrink!
To get a good solution,
The thing we need to do is stop pollution,
Don't wait for a big commotion,
The atmosphere is going to have a big erosion.

Why must mankind be so mean?
The rivers and trees cannot be seen
Because of us being so mean,
People who have asthma might have problems breathing,
This is because of cars giving our fumes,
But if we stop pollution, we will be giving the world a big cleaning!

Burhan Ikram (12)
Hodge Hill Sports & Enterprise College

Here I Am!

Here I am waving my branches,
And there you are,
Taking the sun away from my eyes.

Here I am keeping you alive with my air,
And there you are trying to kill me.

Here I am taking the bad air away from you
And there you are using me for paper.

Here I am minding my own business
And there you are killing me and
My friends and family and their friends
And family as big as Britain.

Samera Saffraz (13)
Hodge Hill Sports & Enterprise College

Help Save The World

The gas, the air, the dust,
All of those things damage the world.

The wars, the racism, the crimes,
All of those things damage the world.

What about clean air?
What about stopping the wars?
What about stopping the racism?

What about all those things?
What about the hurricanes that are damaging the world?
If we don't stop these things,
My world and your world will be in serious danger.

Momin Ahmed Osman (13)
Hodge Hill Sports & Enterprise College

The World's Problem

When they cut the trees,
They go with a bang,
We won't live anymore,
Without them back.

I look at the world,
With all that pollution,
I think to myself,
What's the solution?

Rubbish, litter it's both the same,
Without the trees there's no oxygen,
Why won't people just recycle.

Muhammad Abu-Bakr Arshad (11)
Hodge Hill Sports & Enterprise College

Before

Before
Long ago, before we were here,
When the air was fresh
And the sky was clear,
Animals together they shared,
What they had,
The water, the grass, not one of them sad.

Millions of years past and that's where it started,
Cos poverty, wars and families parted,
You may not believe it but this is all true,
The Earth is dying and it might be because of you.

Rochelle Graham (13)
Hodge Hill Sports & Enterprise College

Our Earth, Our Mother!

Earth, Earth, Earth,
Our great mother,
Life, energy all from her.

Quick, quick, quick,
Saving her,
Damage, pollution around her.

Less, less, less,
Resources and water.

Come on, come on, come on,
Protect our mother.

Mangyuan Lin (14)
Hodge Hill Sports & Enterprise College

Healing The Earth!

The Earth is sick, from all these things:
Smoke, pollution, electricity and for using too much water,
Why can't people ban smoking, dropping litter and start recycling?
Why can't people walk instead of driving, that's what legs are for,
Why do you cut down trees, don't you think we need the oxygen?
The Earth treats us with respect;
Why can't we show respect to the Earth?
Who is going to be responsible, when the Earth is
So sick that she is hopeless?
Who is going to hear her cry?
Crying herself to sleep . . .

Juwairiyah Kauser Khan (11)
Hodge Hill Sports & Enterprise College

The Helpless Earth

The Earth, what should I do?
Nowhere to go, nowhere to hide,
The helpless Earth,
There is no solution to pollution,
Nobody knows, nobody cares,
What should we do people, treat it as nothing?
The Earth is sad, tears start to shed,
Nowhere to go, nowhere to hide,
Today's history, tomorrow's a mystery,
Today's life, tomorrow's death,
What's gonna happen, who knows?

Hameed Gulfraz Hussain (11)
Hodge Hill Sports & Enterprise College

Let's Rescue The World!

Let's rescue the world!
Let's keep it clean,
Let's stop the smoke,
This is no joke,
Let's stop the pollution,
And find a good solution,
For keeping the world clean,
Let's gallop this way,
Let's gallop that way,
Just rescue the world,
Until it's clean.

Faiza Nazir (14)
Hodge Hill Sports & Enterprise College

Healing The Earth

We need to recycle every day,
Everybody will be destroyed while they play,
You need to stop cutting the trees,
Or you will stop breathing,
The Earth will go away.

Don't throw rubbish on the floor,
Or you will die in front of the door,
No more factories,
Or the Earth will turn into a black hole,
Finally the Earth will be destroyed.

Danish Ahmed (11)
Hodge Hill Sports & Enterprise College

Making The World Green

On the ground and in the air,
Pollution spreading everywhere,
Car and planes and smoking too,
Makes life hard for me and you,
So recycle if you can,
Yes, every woman, every man,
Let's work together, you and me,
For a cleaner world for all to see,
We must act now, no time to dream,
Together we can make it green.

Victoria Vaughan (12)
Hodge Hill Sports & Enterprise College

Pollution

Pollution can make you blind,
So don't drive your car,
Ferrari or Lamborghini doesn't matter,
All that matters is the ozone layer.

Lizair Ashraf (12)
Hodge Hill Sports & Enterprise College

Pollution Here And There

Pollution here, pollution there,
Pollution is everywhere,
As we walk around areas,
We would find pollution,
In the houses and down the street,
Pollution becomes so common, you start to weep,
You hear people moan and cry,
Because someone in their family is dying of heart disease,
So help stop pollution,
And come up with a solution.

Melissa Dickens (12)
Hodge Hill Sports & Enterprise College

Our World

The sky is crying,
The Earth is dying,
The plants and animals
Are suffering,
Save the Earth,
Let's save the Earth,
It's our world,
It's our world,
It's our home,
Let's save the world.

Abdul Rahman Al-Harbi (13)
Hodge Hill Sports & Enterprise College

Senses!

I *see* litter pollution,
I *want* to *hear* the birds sing,
I can actually *taste* the blood from people fighting,
I want to *smell* my mom's cooking,
But instead I smell pollution.

Donna Booker (13)
Hodge Hill Sports & Enterprise College

War

We need some new laws,
Which say there must be no more wars,
Because of wars many people have died,
Who in their life have never lied,
Poor families in Africa will tell you,
That unlike British people, they have much to do (hide the truth),
They wake up every morning and travel the road,
And it sounds to me like their life is worse than a toad,
This is all because of war,
And it can be stopped if there was a new life-changing law.

Amir Aziz (12)
Hodge Hill Sports & Enterprise College

Save The World!

The world is a spectacular place,
Exactly like a race,
When it starts, it has to end,
But I will need the help of a friend,
So why don't you be the one,
Help me out on the crack of dawn,
Let's find a solution,
To stop this pollution,
And bring it to an end,
So we can be with a friend.

Nazmin Begum (15)
Hodge Hill Sports & Enterprise College

Earth

E arth is getting too weak,
A nimals are going to be extinct,
R ecycling is going in the bin,
T echnology has been a sin,
H ave a heart, save the Earth.

Arron Nicholls (13)
Hodge Hill Sports & Enterprise College

Earth

Our Earth, stop the bleeding,
Stop the killing, stop the polluting and more,
Our Earth will get sore.

Through blood, through pains and through sorrow,
Now we can see we cannot borrow,
Look at the time and people doing crime,
In four years time, our Earth will be gone.

Our Earth is fading before us,
Stop everything including the fuss.

Abdullah Khan (13)
Hodge Hill Sports & Enterprise College

Untitled

Saving the world is important because everybody could die,
There's too much pollution everywhere,
There must be a solution for all this pollution,
And there could be a revolution,
There is a disaster, there's going to be a cry faster,
There's too much rubbish on the floor,
Pick it up and put it in the bins and don't touch the tins,
These lot of people causing global warming by sprays,
And sailors throwing all thanks in seas.

Kasim Rehman (12)
Hodge Hill Sports & Enterprise College

Earth Is Dying

Earth is dying,
We need to keep on trying,
The revelation is coming,
The pollution is spreading,
Save the Earth,
Because this is our turf!

Reace Lynch (13)
Hodge Hill Sports & Enterprise College

Green

Grass is good,
Plants are good,
Woods are good,
Forests are good,
Racism is . . .
Pollution is . . .
Terrorists are . . .
Cars are . . .
The world is full of unwanted gaps.

Haider Ali Khattak (15)
Hodge Hill Sports & Enterprise College

Love

Love is needed,
Love is something you want,
Love is also something you cherish,
It lives close to your heart,
You will always find it when you need it,
It will always be with you to save your life,
Whatever the matter is:
It's there for you,
Love *everyone!*

Ravina Parmar (15)
Hodge Hill Sports & Enterprise College

Healing The Earth

The Earth is sick, sick, sick,
We need to help it quick, quick, quick,
Or it will be hated and we will be disappointed,
Recycle paper or we will be in a load of danger,
Don't cause pollution or we will be unsafe,
Don't pollute the Earth, it has the right to stay clean,
Don't be mean.

Mohammed Kabeel (11)
Hodge Hill Sports & Enterprise College

Planet Earth

The Earth is going round but the oil spills are going bad,
As the boats go around killing sea animals and plants,
Global warming going mad, if we all help, we can fight it back,
The ice is melting away as we will very soon,
As the cars go by,
The pollution level is going high,
The animals are getting killed for skin
Or for other animals, locked away in zoos
As hunters are on the move.

Ibrahim Rasool (11)
Hodge Hill Sports & Enterprise College

Healing The Earth

We all must recycle our paper, paper, paper,
We must not throw our litter, litter, litter,
We all treat animals nicely, nicely, nicely,
We don't waste water, water, water,
Trees give us oxygen, oxygen, oxygen,
We don't waste electricity, electricity, electricity,
We need to help him quick, quick, quick,
Before we are in danger, danger, danger,
The Earth is sick, sick, sick.

Zamir Ahmed (11)
Hodge Hill Sports & Enterprise College

The World

The Earth is dying slowly,
Like a withering flower,
Man was given something,
So pure but is selfishly destroying it,
With their greed and lust for power,
Man is slowly destroying himself with ignorance,
Depriving innocent species of life.

Liam O'Sullivan (15)
Hodge Hill Sports & Enterprise College

Reduce, Recycle, Reuse

The world is overflowing, global warming is a problem,
Stop pounding the ground with waste,
Reduce waste and upgrade to recycling,
So reduce, reuse and recycle.

The habitats of animals are dying,
Humans can't bear the heat,
Ice caps are melting and seas rising,
So reduce, reuse and recycle.

Moin Rehman (11)
Hodge Hill Sports & Enterprise College

Untitled

This is a warming,
About global warming,
The Earth will slowly die away,
If we don't make a change today.

Recycle more, don't use cars,
Recycle more things like glass jars,
Save energy by turning off the light,
Turn off all the plugs at night.

Ryan Moules (11)
Hodge Hill Sports & Enterprise College

The World Is Changing

The world is changing,
Climate change, pollution and waste,
So reduce, reuse, recycle,
You don't drive, you cycle,
No matter where or even when,
Cycling is a safe way for our world,
And now is the time we need to
Work together!

Thomas Godwin (12)
Hodge Hill Sports & Enterprise College

Homeless People

Poor people pay for poverty,
They become as skinny as skeletons,
They starve and have no home,
Poor people are all alone.

We can help if we donate,
We can help if we are their mate,
Donate food, clothing and money,
If we help the world it will be sunny!

Bilaal Mansab (11)
Hodge Hill Sports & Enterprise College

Green, Green Don't Be Mean

Green, green don't be mean,
Keep our world nice and clean,
Use a bus instead of a car,
It is cheaper and will take you far.

Turn your lights off, it will help,
Or the world will give a great big yelp,
The world is burning, the world is dying,
That's because we're not helping.

Farhead Ali Meghal (12)
Hodge Hill Sports & Enterprise College

Saving The Earth!

Throw all rubbish in the bin,
But don't try and sneak it in the biscuit tins,
Try a run or maybe a jog,
It's not just saving you, it's saving everything we do,
The Earth is a big smashed screen,
Can you please do something that you really mean.
We can all do our bit to save a pound or two,
But people do really know what to do.

Saiqa Hussain (12)
Hodge Hill Sports & Enterprise College

That Affects Us All

Say no to drugs,
Say no to war,
Say no to pollution,
That affects us all.

Say yes to peace,
And heed the call,
And save this world,
That affects us all.

Lauren Evans (13)
Hodge Hill Sports & Enterprise College

Saving The World

Stop the car smoke,
Before we choke,
Leave it green,
Don't be mean,
Leave the forest,
Let it flourish,
The end will be near,
So come on, let's clear.

Melissa Miller (14)
Hodge Hill Sports & Enterprise College

Earth

E lectricity giving off power plant gases,
A ll the people who are doing crime,
    Can't you see that it is a waste of time,
R ivers streaming down now,
    They've all got tyres and a little girl's gown,
T here is a better place for me and you,
    Stop global warming and you will see too,
H ere we are glanced beyond the stars.

Imran Saleem (13)
Hodge Hill Sports & Enterprise College

The Earth Is In Danger

The Earth is sick, sick, sick,
We need to do something quick, quick, quick,
Don't waste water, water, water,
Save some for your daughter, daughter, daughter,
So help the Earth, Earth, Earth,
She needs us now, now, now,
I know you can, can, can,
I know you know how, how, how!

Jack Lewis (11)
Hodge Hill Sports & Enterprise College

Healing The Earth

The Earth is a globe, don't pollute the world,
Or destroy the trees, please, please, please,
Don't cut off the oxygen, or you will suffer,
If you don't think.

Stop all destruction, recycle for the world,
Don't hurt it anymore,
Look after our world!

Myron Drummond (11)
Hodge Hill Sports & Enterprise College

The Earth Is Sick

The Earth is dying because of pollution,
The Earth is sick so help us quick.

E arth is crying out
A nimals are dying out,
R ecycle your waste,
T rees are getting cut down,
H elp us to save the Earth.

Liam Sean Burke (13)
Hodge Hill Sports & Enterprise College

Why Smoke? It's Not A Joke!

Smoking drugs is so bad,
Sometimes it makes people go mad,
And then their parents will feel so sad,
It isn't a joke, people will die or choke,
Everyone has just spoke,
It causes pollution,
We have to solve this with a scary solution.

Mohammed Ali Hussain (13)
Hodge Hill Sports & Enterprise College

Saving The Earth

Stop driving your car to work,
Get on your bike and cycle to work,
Stop lurking around the corner going for a kill,
Go free range and stop killing
And stop littering all over the place,
So get off your bum and put it in the bin,
Please save the world for the future.

Thomas Marson (11)
Hodge Hill Sports & Enterprise College

Bit By Bit

Polar ice caps are melting bit by bit,
We killed animals bit by bit,
So why won't you help them, bit by bit?
Days are getting shorter and days are getting hotter,
Can you help?
Won't you help?
Will you help?

Shadab Iqbal (12)
Hodge Hill Sports & Enterprise College

Chilling

Let's save the Earth because it's ours,
Chilling shouldn't be the only thing on our mind.

So let's get together and save poverty,
And live with the assurance of people being safe.

With this we will gain the peace of mind,
That we can all live a good life as long as we try.

Haider Ali (15)
Hodge Hill Sports & Enterprise College

Earth Should Be Clean

E veryone must try to be clean,
A lways try to be helpful and clean,
R ight or wrong, try to be strong,
T his is the way,
H ow life will be OK.

Saira Rashid (13)
Hodge Hill Sports & Enterprise College

Global Warming

The world is ending,
Global warming is ruining.
The sun looking so small,
But feeling so powerful.
Destroying our world
Minute by minute.

Do we want to end this?
Yes we do!
Then let's put our hands together,
Fight against this monster
And victory shall be ours.

Huja Sallah (12)
Holyhead School

Round And Round The World I Go

As the sun rises with a pure light
Trees awake whilst mountains rise,
The moon settles clear and low,
As the breeze stirs the air with a gentle flow.

The Earth weakens every day,
By litter and pollution there is much to say,
To nature this is a disgrace
And many find it hard to face.

All litter you should bin it,
Trees crying whilst plants dying,
All nature destroying under minute,
Round and round the world I go.

Round and round the world I go
As the ball of gas above us all
Shines brightly, clear and small.

Round and round the world I go
As the silver claw sets its way
To give its moonlight every day.

Serena Kaur Bains
Holyhead School

Pollution

Pollution, what a terrible thing
Pollution makes the world sink
For a solution to stop pollution
Pollution needs to be minimised
People around the world should open their eyes
Don't wait for it to get worse
The ozone is about to burst.

Simranjeet Kaur Bhurjee
Holyhead School

82

Do Something

The Earth was made for a people to live in
When petrol prices went up you carried on using it
You did nothing
You make him angry.

This is your crime
Now you live in gases and fumes
Polluted air
You are now responsible for those with illness
You ruined their life.

You may be thinking what the crime was
Well pay the fine.

Recycling paper is not that much
Throwing your litter away is also so much
Be green or pay the crime
You can make a difference
Make a change or pay.

Chirag Patel (11)
Holyhead School

Green

G o and save energy because
R ealistically,
E verybody is going to die if you ignore
E verything, like: recycling, power saving light bulbs etc.
N o one will exist if you don't do your bit.

James Phillips (12)
King Edward VI Five Ways School

Animals' Lives

Animals are all around
From the sky to the ground,
They play with you
And help you too.

So do they deserve imprisonment
In your home
Or in the zoo
When they want to be wild?

When you're hunting
Are you thinking
About the lives you're killing?
What's the point?

We take advantage
Of the poor creatures,
Buying them to eat
And wearing their skin.

Have you ever polluted the sea?
Thinking what it would do,
Killing or harming a fish
And for what?

Blowing up land,
Cutting down a forest,
What is really happening?
A home is being destroyed.

All of this is helping,
Helping to cause extinction,
But do you really mean it to?
Ever so slowly they're fading away.

All you have to do
Is throw away your rubbish.
Everyone can make a difference,
By doing a little.

Don't hunt for greed
Or your treasures,
Do you really need
A deer on your wall?

Save the land,
Recycle all you can

Then less forests will be cut,
Save the animals' homes.

If you do your bit
Others will follow,
As long as you help
Remember act local,
Think global!

Thomas Mayers (13)
Lyndon School

Rainforest Song

Waiting for the moon to appear before us
And watching the sun hide underneath the trees,
We all fly above and over, humming our tune
As we join the rainforest medley.

Beginning with the insects
Which carpet the forest floor,
Then followed by the monkeys
Who can play no more.

All this noise is like the machines that came before
But it all stops as I begin my song,
Until an uproar of singing
Shows that we remain strong.

That is until the howler monkey sounds
And our tune comes to a stop,
As men and machine advance on us
Taking the trees with a chop.

This machine is a monster
Cutting down our home,
Destroying all our memories
And all we've ever known.

I was a lucky one
To escape from what is wrong,
But in my new home, all is silent
Because there is no rainforest song.

Daniel Maddison (13)
Lyndon School

Makes The World What It Is

To beckon your freedom,
To kick out the clouds,
To make your home, Son,
And not hear a sound.
All the colours of the world
Make the world what it is.
But the past comes back
When there was no mixing
And the anxious faces think
But don't say, *this needs fixing.*
It was alright back then, Son,
They didn't know any better,
But you choose, you write,
Your page, your letter.
You make sure you're not one of them,
Causing riot and fear but you'll show them, Son
When you're the sunflower and they're still the seed.
It's not how it used to be,
But it's become better, but
There's always the odd one out,
The sad little fretter.

To beckon your culture
And be part of a race,
There's only one you need to know of,
It's human, everybody's got that fate.
So you can stand back
And laugh, Son,
When they make a comment
But they'll never know, Son,
The plan, the summit.
All the colours in the world,
Make the world want it is.
White, black, yellow and brown,
Even if it is the colour of your skin.

Tahmina Begum (13)
Lyndon School

The Story Of The Great War

Years of waiting
For the ceasefire
As the soldiers death toll
Grows higher and higher.

In 1914 came
The start of World War I
It wasn't until four years later
That the fighting was done.

The war on the Western Front
German versus British and French
Four years of fighting for what?
A few metres of a ground and another trench.

In the desolate area
Of Flanders, Northern France,
Boom, boom, boom go millions of guns.
Who has a living chance?

By 11am on 11/11/18
Millions had already died
And only after the madness
People thought, *why?*

After World War I
The world said, 'No more'
But the Great War solved nothing
And just led to the Second World War.

Joseph Benton (13)
Lyndon School

Lights

L ook before you turn them on
I don't ignore that it's wrong
G et the bulbs that save energy
H ate it but live with it
T he Earth will spin forever
S o save energy.

Rebecca Tovey (11)
Lyndon School

Be Green, Be Happy!

Too many cars,
Too much pollution,

Too many people,
Too little money,

Blood, guts and gore,
We need to stop war,

Too much litter,
Not enough bins,

Lots of trees,
Not anymore,

Wasting electricity,
Coal running low,

Rare animals,
Going extinct,

You have to help us,
Make it better,

Cut down on electricity,
Save more money,
Be green, be happy!

Help our world,
Don't hinder it.

Mollie White (11)
Lyndon School

Go Green

G o and put your rubbish in a bin
O r recycle

G et less rubbish in the street
R ecycle as much as you can
E nergy save
E very time you leave a room turn the light off
N ever leave things left on.

Jack Lewis (12)
Lyndon School

88

Together We Can Make It Better!

I can hear their
screams every
day and night.

Those painful
cries making
me fight.

Against those
people who think
it's fun
to have wars against
innocent ones.

Our green world
is turning red
creating poverty
and a lot of mess.

If we work
together somehow
we can save the
world right now.

Mashal Ahmed (11)
Lyndon School

The Tiger

T he bone cruncher beast
I nvincible creature
G reat jaws
E normous fangs
R ighteous speed.

The tiger is endangered.
The bone cruncher beast is now a figure of memory.
The invincible creature is no more.
Its great jaws are nothing but dust -
Enormous fangs hang in the museum -
Righteous speed comes to an *end*.

Harry Marsh & Tahmid Rahmid (11)
Lyndon School

Rainforest Terror

Chop, chop, chop,
Thump, crash, thump, crash,
There goes another tree.
Heads . . .
All I can hear is a faint echo,
Bang, crash, bang, bang, bang, bang,
Squeals and cries can be heard,
Homeless endangered animals flee.
Crash!
Another one bites the dust.
I inhale the smoke-infested air.
I follow the thick grey suffocating cloud,
Crackle, crackle, crackle.
Am I home?
I come to an opening where they're burning dead trunks.
Fire, fire, fire,
I faint from the heat.
My eyes open early, I'm back in my bedroom!
I must . . .
Recycle, recycle, recycle.

Bethany Grace Thomas (13)
Lyndon School

Rats

So much pollution can be seen,
Also can be used.

Litter everywhere I go, I try and clean it up
But it comes and goes.

I hear things rattle on the ground,
Is it a squawking, rattling sound?

I try again and then I hear a *bang!* as I fall,
Will this be the end or will there be more?
I lie there silently across the floor,
Will there be another door?

Laura Freeman (11)
Lyndon School

90

Wonderful World

In the calm Arctic the polar bear prowls through the icy landscape,
minding their own business, making the white blanket of snow look even more
beautiful.
The only life for miles.
The echo of his roar surrounds the empty white world.
Why would we give that up?

In the reckless rainforest, the orang-utan swings from branch to branch
through the tall treetops making the most of the gorgeous green world around
them like a child in a toy store.
The screech of them playing and laughing makes the colourful birds flutter
away in a swarm from the sky-high canopies.
Why would we give that up?

In the deep blue sea the shark slivers and sways through the waves searching
for prey at every angle.
His magnificent beady eyes move back and forth in a sly-like manner.
The area is emptied as all the sea creatures dash at the sight of the huge great
white.
He makes it clear to all he is the king of the sea.
Why would we give it up?

Ashleigh Newnes (13)
Lyndon School

Young War

Marching through the town,
Friends and family crying, comforting each other.
Dressed in khaki and black,
Wearing black shiny boots.
They think about their battles ahead,
About how many will live,
And how many will die.
Yes, they're scared, apprehensive and uneasy,
But these young soldiers
Are their country's last hope.
Their last hope of winning the war.

Hayley Boswell (14)
Lyndon School

One Single Blink

I opened my mind
And started to think
If the world could change,
In one single blink.

Everyone's happy,
We're all hand in hand,
None of us listening
To anyone's demand.

Proud of who we are
From black to white,
Fighting off racism
With all of our might.

I opened my mind
And started to think
That the world cannot change
In one single blink.

Léa Campbell (13)
Lyndon School

Racism

Racism, racism
Doesn't it hurt
To feel so alone and be treated like dirt?
Racism, racism
It's only a colour,
Black is black
And white is white,
Just like any other.
Racism, racism
In the playground or on the street
Discriminating people because they're unique.
Racism, racism
Don't exclude others,
Treat them how you want to be treated
Like a sister or a brother.

Bethany Witcomb (13)
Lyndon School

Untitled

When I started off I was just a ball of burning rock,
I produced water for fishes to live in
But now it has all changed, people treat me like a bin.

I can't take this damage anymore, don't turn your back on me,
I won't be ignored,
Time won't take . . .
I won't be ignored.

People turn their lights on in their warm and snuggly homes,
I am boiling like a bunch of live volcano stones,
I have so many different colours, and so many different tones,
People are digging down so low, they're gonna reach my bones.

I can't take this damage anymore, don't turn your back on me,
I won't be ignored,
Time won't take . . .
I won't be ignored.

Tom Hogan (11) & Kaylan Hamilton (12)
Lyndon School

The Earth's Lament

I can feel the weight building,
My skin is burning,
I can't control it.
I'm getting hotter and hotter,
But what can I do?

Chunks of my body are being picked,
Being destroyed and used,
I can't control it.
My friends are shrinking,
But what can I do?

I'm dying, bit by bit,
Slowly dissolving,
I can't control it,
I am the Earth,
But what can I do?

Lauren Cotterill (11)
Lyndon School

What Is Happening To Our World?

What is happening to our world?
What is happening to our world?
What has happened to the fresh air?
What has happened to the green grass?

What will happen to our future?
Will the world continue like this?

So much pollution,
Is this the destiny of our world?

So much mess,
Will it ever reduce?

All the cars, factories, misuse of bins!
All this trouble . . . why?

So much to do!
So little time!

Zahra Aurangzeb (12)
Lyndon School

Trees

T eams
R ecycle
E cosystem
E nvironment
S afety.

We give you oxygen
You give us a frown.
We give you energy
And you cut us down.
You cut us down
And we make paper
And you come back again a little later.
So go ahead and cut us down
But just remember don't give us a frown.

Remy Moore & Lauren Amys (11)
Lyndon School

Ozone Layer

The ozone layer is burning away
Earth's core is getting hotter by the minute
It's time to take action today
The people of Earth just bin it
If they don't need it.

Obviously people will not care
If I fly up into outer space
If to kill an animal is a dare
Think about the time and place.

The sun is boiling up
I just want you to know
Wherever you are in the world
You can't hide from the ozone layer.

Rebecca Boswell (11)
Lyndon School

Out There!

'You're not the same as me, you're black, I'm white, go away.'
I felt alone, an outsider.
My words dropped to my feet.
Speechless, frozen, hurt.
I get racism all the time, I feel ashamed of my colour,
My culture, my beliefs.

Try being me for a day,
Broken, depressed, totally fed up.
What's the problem with my skin colour?
White, black, other,
It's just something that we live in.
Inside we're all the same,
So tell me racism, what's there to gain!

Kerry Morton (14)
Lyndon School

Death

War is a sad place
They sit all day in a base
When they go to bed
They will soon end up dead

The wars are wrong
Maybe we should sing a song
Then the guns will go off
Then the men will make their last cough

People always die
We should all say bye
When we get on the battlefield
They will soon be killed.

Alex Harrison (14)
Lyndon School

Earth

Hurt by slow digging,
Being used up,
Water starting to poison me,
Only a young pup.

Wildlife slowly dying,
Pollution, litter, waste,
Chemicals are really nasty,
Not a very nice taste.

Humans just use, use, use,
Never give any back,
Some humans try to help me,
The rest are all slack.

Daniel Weaver (11)
Lyndon School

Do Your Bit

Around the world, oil's running dry,
It's causing lots of wars,
It's causing lots of pollution
And I think we know the cause.

It's huge rainforests being ripped apart
And our parent's brand new car,
And all because we can't be bothered
To put on a coat and walk that far.

If we all picked up some litter
And recycled like we care,
Then we can put an end
To this real life nightmare.

Molly McGinn (13)
Lyndon School

Why?

What has the world come to?
There is too much going on!

When you look up to the sky
What you see will soon be gone.

With all the pollution and climate change
There will be no more you and me.

All the people in Africa who have
No dinner or tea,

Why is this going on? Just stop it now!
I'm prepared to take control
And I will make a stand!

Charlotte Coy (12)
Lyndon School

The Earth

Has the Earth become what it shouldn't be?
Is it making life hard for you and me?
Litter, climate change and pollution,
If we put our heads together there is a solution.
So to stop the wrong and make it right,
Should we work hard all day and night?
Let's make the Earth happy and glad
And leave behind the days that are boring and sad.
We can help, so let's make a difference
And make our future bright and different.

Sara Powell (11)
Lyndon School

If I Could Turn Back Time

If I could smell the world it would smell like burning flames
And fumes and the stench of the old long-lost river.

If I could touch the world it would be as hot as a volcano
And crumbling in my hands like burnt toast left cooking for centuries.

If I could hear the world I would hear the sound of screaming animals
And the plea of humans begging for their lives.

But if I could see the world it would be flooded and full of pollution
And left with parts from the old world that did not deserve this . . .

Anthony Lloyd (12)
Lyndon School

Black Or White

Racism, it's a form of discrimination.
Racism, we are God's greatest creation.
If you're white as a whiteboard,
Black as the night,
It doesn't matter if you're black or white.

Ben Blakeman (13)
Lyndon School

98

Pollution

P ollution is a bad thing
O ur ozone layer is being destroyed
L ife is changing for all of us
L iving on Earth is getting harder
U niverse is dying
T ragedy
I feel terrible
O ur planet is getting worse and worse
N othing will ever change.

Nikhil Vadukul (11)
Lyndon School

War

War's a white lily, it's too silly, just hearing it makes me chilly.
It makes people sad, that proves it is bad.
People drop down, it is horrible, can't you see?
Kamikaze, it's suicide when it touches my eyes,
It must be lies but it's not a plot
And I say no, it's one bad shot.
The families are crying because their husbands are dying
But really I don't know why.
It's war against the law.

Stuart Bateman (12)
Lyndon School

Racism Hurts

People scared to step outside.
Scared of people making them cry.
White is white.
Black is black.
It doesn't matter what you are,
Everybody should have an equal chance.

Charlie Simpson (13)
Lyndon School

Pollution

P ollution is a bad thing
O ur ozone layer is being destroyed
L ife on Earth will die out
L ife is changing for all of
U s
T ime is changing, we must stop it
I n, time seasons will change
O ur planet can't cope with it
N othing will happen unless we change our actions.

Ariful Islam (11)
Lyndon School

The Earth

The Earth has become what it shouldn't be,
Making life harder for you and me.
Litter, climate change and pollution,
If we put our heads together there is a solution.
To stop the wrong and make it right
We work hard day and night.
So let's make the Earth happy and glad
And leave behind days that are boring and sad.

Apeksha Gandhi (11)
Lyndon School

I've Got Words

I've got words, I've got words about war,
Words about racism and so much more.
I've got words, animals, extinction and poverty.
I've got words to describe the dead rainforest.
I've got words, words about recycling.
I've got words, climate change on the rise,
Being homeless comes as a great surprise.
I've got words, please save our planet from extinction.

Jay Douglas (12)
Lyndon School

Help!

We always hear that people need help,
They're homeless, they're moneyless,
Children sleeping in poverty and litter.
Always hearing racist comments,
Starving people and death all around them,
Oh please help,
They need a helping hand to bring their life back.
Help, please help!

Elizabeth Rayner
Lyndon School

Climate Change

Climate change threatens us and the wildlife around the world
The energy is too much for the world to cope
Bad weather land to sea
We need to give a helping hand
Recycling paper, plastic and cardboard boxes
Animals can't survive the dreadful toxics
Help us change, climate change
Help, help, help the Earth!

Kayley Duffy (13)
Lyndon School

Litter

Litter is a troubled thing
I know it needs to stop
There are people helping
There are people who are not
Everyone should want a cleaner world
Realise what you're doing to help!

Liam Brooks (12)
Lyndon School

All We Can Do Is Dream!

Sitting in my classroom,
Listening to tales of doom,
A thought popped into my mind,
How many ways to help can I find . . .

A normal boring day,
Soon filled with life,
Thoughts soon were buzzing,
Messing with my brain.

A world of misery,
Soon descending,
Hopes of love and happiness,
Long gone away.

As I write,
My hand is shaking,
My heart breaking,
I cannot make this fear disappear.

War is not a pleasant thing,
Life at a standstill,
People still cry over the lost,
The ones whom I have to thank.

One engraved memory,
Haunting all those,
Who lived the fear of many,
And still hear the siren call.

Why can't peace rule the world?
Not a leader throughout,
A hero or heroine leading the way,
To a better place, no doubt.

Racism is part of war,
A dreaded hate towards many,
A race is a race,
But everyone has a heart.

You may have to look deep,
Beneath the long-lost heart,
To find a part of warmth and joy,
Where there is happiness for all.

All we can do is dream!

Amy Timms (12)
Lyng Hall School

Animals Have Feelings

Animals are colourful,
Animals are bright,
But when they become extinct
It is not right.

We're killing animals every day,
Oh no they're going away,
Too bad we can't watch them stroll around,
We only see them touch the ground.

Tiger and pandas,
Rhinos and gorillas,
They're all endangered,
Workers killing them, eating tortillas.

Help us please
To help animals,
Herbivores, omnivores, carnivores
And even cannibals.

We are all animals,
We don't care,
What about nature,
They do care.

Coist David Bary Evans (12)
Lyng Hall School

Racism

R acism,
A ll around the world different
C olours and religions
I n different countries. We're the
S ame inside. We are all part of
M ankind.

Joshua Parsons (13)
Lyng Hall School

Be Environmentally Friendly

Pollution is a majorly destructive hurricane,
It contains diseases which could make your life end in a full stop.
Being homeless is really hard
And to stop pollution you can recycle things like card.
Racism leads to devastation which ends up with revenge.
War is caused by racism, so is pollution.
Litter is made by people,
But everyone would suffer in pain now or later.
Innocent animals get killed on a daily basis,
Finally they become extinct and they stop their innocent chases,
The rainforests die
Which means the animals have to say bye-bye.
Do you think you can make the world a better place?
Have you done enough?
Do you want to help the innocent people who are suffering
From diseases caused by pollution?

Recycle, avoid racism, stop pollution
Is what we should do.

Pavithran Devaharan (12)
Lyng Hall School

The Big Green Poem

Vietnam is where we lie,
Do not enter or you may die.
If you wish to be dead
Vietnam is your deathbed.

Time and money is what we spend,
Now we must stop and try and mend.
What we are creating is pollution,
If we work together we can find the solution.

We must all learn to try and share,
It is a simple way to show we care.
To save the world love is the key,
Help is needed to save you and me.

Jordon Newbold (12)
Lyng Hall School

What Next?

Fields of green glistening grass
Across the sunlit field,
It's like a destiny
Waiting for something to happen.
We have so much,
Wait and think of the unfortunate,
Poorer or richer it doesn't matter.
Rain spreading harshly like never before,
Recycle, then will people be happy?
Put yourself in the positive,
No animal testing or hunting
Killing our precious wildlife,
No recycling means we use machines to make things.
Polluting Earth,
People cutting down trees.
What next?
We are all individuals.

Traé O'Sullivan (12)
Lyng Hall School

What About The World?

Poverty . . .
People dying endlessly, one after another.
Diseases, starvation, illnesses, racism - all problems we can solve.
All over the world people suffer.
Everyone is equal and should be respected and treated in the same way.
No matter how you are: beautiful or small, ugly or tall,
You are the same as everyone else.
No one's perfect, everyone makes mistakes - it's part of life!

Global warming . . .
What's the point of littering and polluting the Earth,
It only brings bad causes eg natural disasters, cyclones,
Aftershocks, hurricanes, tornadoes, floods, storms, tsunamis etc.
If we recycle the world will be much healthier and happier!
Treat everything as how you would like to be treated.

Orinder Nagra (13)
Lyng Hall School

Please May You Stop

The environment is destroyed,
Why can't you help me?
Stop chucking stuff
On the floor.
Why do you have to chop down
Every tree that you see?
Stop dropping litter
And turn on the TV
And listen to the news,
People are trying to say stuff to you.
Stop and listen now if you care,
People are dying
Every seventeen seconds.
You could be saving
People's lives right now,
So be careful
About what you do.

Katy Williams (11)
Lyng Hall School

The World At Its End

Trees being cut down,
Habitats being moved around,
Animals having nowhere to stay,
Slowly they are dying away.

We need to keep our lush green leaves
So we have enough oxygen to breathe.
One life, one chance,
Save the animals, save the plants.

Stop this before the world ends,
Tell your family, tell your friends.
Change this before it's too late,
Then we won't face a horrible fate!

Sameenah Begum (13)
Lyng Hall School

Make The World Green Again

We hear about the world going less green,
The emerald-green trees,
Now so grey and dull,
All getting cut down,
Although they should be still up.

There is also the pollution,
Cars giving out fumes,
People should rather be walking, or taking bikes or buses.
People should help the world,
Before it's all dead and dull.

There is not just these two,
There is also war, poverty and climate change,
There's many things,
But just one of us helping the world,
Is not enough,
We all need to help this world so it turns green again.

Nisha Hayre (12)
Lyng Hall School

Difference!

Turn on the TV,
Look what you can see.

You can make a difference,
So recycle bottles and glass.

Turn off things when you pass,
You can make a difference.

Pay a small amount,
You can save thousands of people.

So turn off the TV
And make a difference!

Gemma Yeomans (11)
Lyng Hall School

Untitled

Recycling is good,
It won't cause a flood,
Water is good,
It is in my blood,
Saving children's life,
Do not give them the knife,
Do not litter,
You won't get fitter,
Walk to school,
Don't be a fool,
Children are sad,
Don't be so bad,
Walk to work,
Don't give a smirk,
Last of all, acid rain,
It causes a lot of *pain!*

Aarron Somal (11)
Lyng Hall School

Extinction

E very animal has a home
eX cept when the hunters come around
   T hey rip and they smash, they shoot and they bound
   I nto the animals' homes
N one left after they've been
C ounting down the animals left
T ill there are no more
   I n the animal world
O ver and over they do it again
N ow no more animals left.

Jordan Tuxford (12)
Lyng Hall School

Recycle

Recycle, do your bit for the community,
Why don't you recycle?
R e c y c l e, what does that spell? Recycle.
When you're walking down the street
And you see some rubbish, pick it up
And put it in the bin.
Yer, yer, yer recycle,
It's not that hard,
Recycle.

Kalisha Greaves (11)
Lyng Hall School

Go Green

Green,
Not as a colour,
But as a way to change,
Recycle,
Walk,
Turn it off,
Help the world,
Stop it dying,
Go green.

Laura-Rose Goldsmith (12)
Lyng Hall School

Recycle Dude!

R ecycle everything
E verything can be recycled
C an you make a robot?
Y ou can make a dinosaur out of milk bottles
C reativity is the key
L ike the Earth
E arth rules!

Sulaiman Choudhury (12)
Lyng Hall School

Don't Be Greedy!

Don't be greedy,
Help the needy,
Frozen cold,
Homeless children,
No water,
Nor food,
Hungry, thirsty,
Give them food.

Rosie Cunningham (12)
Lyng Hall School

Untitled

Keep it clean,
Make it green.
Walking in the countryside
Is nice to be seen.
Pollution in the air,
Nobody's being fair.
What about our health?
All people think about is wealth.

Charlotte Scully (13)
Lyng Hall School

Be Clean Not Mean!

Be clean,
Don't be mean,
The environment
Will turn to punishment,
So listen 'cause
We want to make the Earth glisten
So clean up your litter,
Be the environment's babysitter.

Saskia Naylor (11)
Lyng Hall School

Save A Life

Save a child's life,
How good will you feel,
Just save a life.
A life of an innocent child,
Dies every day,
How bad will you feel
If you did not even save one life?
Save a child's life.

Saqib Ishaq (11)
Lyng Hall School

Skittles Packet

Yummy, tasty, soft in your mouth,
Sweet and lovely makes you feel good.

Smooth, chewy like a soft angel,
Nice and kind,
You want more, you wish you could.

Enjoy it while you can,
It's over, time to throw it in the bin.

Emma Louise Lawson (14)
Lyng Hall School

Untitled

Help the children's lives,
Give them sweet honey from the beehives.
Don't litter, it is giving the world pollution,
There must be a solution.
Don't put litter in the sea,
The animals think it's their tea.

Amy-Victoria Goldsmith (11)
Lyng Hall School

Pollution

Pollution on Earth is really bad,
I am surprised people aren't getting mad!

Let's stop pollution and make a change . . .
Do something for the world just like an exchange.

Let's stop pollution for a great life!

Tyler Williams (12)
Lyng Hall School

Tree

T rees are so great
R eally they should be safe
E lm trees, palm trees, oak trees and more
E verybody save a tree just for me.

Josh Gardner (11)
Lyng Hall School

Yesterday

Just yesterday it seemed the
Fields were full of grain.

Just yesterday, the water was fresh
And the Earth was not dying of thirst.

But yesterday is ten years gone
And today there is nothing.
No longer is it peace, instead it's wild,
Baked black by the restless, burning desert sun.
Now fires spread with rage,
Is it still Planet Earth or is it a miserable cage . . .?

Sahabah Ahmed (12)
Selly Park Technology College

The Big Green Poetry Machine

I'm big, I'm green,
I'm the poetry machine,
I'm smelly, I'm loud,
No pollution is allowed,
Cos I'm big, I'm green,
Everything has to be clean.

I clean up your rubbish,
Please no more racism,
There I see a homeless person,
I think I could help them,
I'm big, I'm green,
I'm the poetry machine.

Cars driving past,
All it takes is one walk,
Just think of the homeless,
They can hardly talk,
But, I'm big, I'm green,
I'm the poetry machine.

But as for animal extinction
There is no need,
Why not help them out?
It would be a good deed,
I'll help, cos I'm big, I'm green,
I'm the poetry machine.

Everywhere I go,
I see more litter.
That's what bins are for,
Why be so bitter?
I'm big, I'm green,
I'm the poetry machine.

So now I'll say goodbye,
I hope you took it in,
Maybe now we shall clean,
It isn't so boring,
I'm big, I'm green,
I'm the one and only poetry machine.

Samantha White (13)
Selly Park Technology College

Environment Poem

In 2019 where will you be?
Will you be at home or history?
It's up to you, which one?
Do you want to live in a nice environment
Or one that you destroyed?

It's up to you,
Think carefully on what you throw in the bin.
Can you recycle or use it as scrap?
Think which box you shall put it in!

Stop polluting!
Drive less!
Don't litter!
Don't be a pest!

People all over the world die from heat waves
And from the freezing cold!
Do you want this to happen?
You can make a difference!

Start now! Do your part!
Don't leave it to everyone else! Have a heart!
Don't you care about the world and everyone in it?
Do you enjoy polluting? Doing things, people
Are trying to prevent in the world?

Stop now if your answer is yes!
If your answer is no, then carry on recycling!
Don't copy the people who pollute!
Don't litter. Do your part.

In 2019 where will you be?
Will you be at home or history?
It's up to you, it's your decision!
Don't let people die because you're polluting!
Stop! Think about the Earth and everyone in it!
Is what you are doing helping
Or making things worse?

Just think and ask yourself this,
When you have lived your life on this Earth,
Will it be better, because you lived?
Think. Do your part to help.

Rafia Javaid (12)
Selly Park Technology College

114

Global Warming

All our worldly green is going
But our fuel demands keep growing
Sea levels rise up from the rim
And instead of walking we will have to swim.

While Mother Nature cries out
With excruciating pain
We sit around and mope about
The sun and then the rain.

Our world is dying young
From devastation we have brought
And while nature sweats away
We pollute throughout the day.

But did we ever stop to think?
Did we ever make the link?
That it's the fault of all of us
That brought the world to craziness.

We could always save the day
We could always turn away
From adding to the blanket
That surrounds us day and night
That keeps in all the warm
But lets out all the light.

So recycle, reuse
And please do not abuse
The world has always been our friend
So let's repay the loyalty
And stop it from the sorrowful end.

Sanna Rauf (13)
Selly Park Technology College

Our Planet

I once thought what I did didn't matter at all,
But then I found the world was really quite small.
The whole world is affected by the actions I take;
I never knew what a difference one person could make.
Something as simple as turning off a light
Is a step toward saving the world from its plight.
If you put it all together it'll add up really fast
And then maybe our days on this planet will last.
At the rate we're going now we don't have very long,
But I'm convinced those who call it hopeless are wrong.
If we all work together then we can succeed
At saving ourselves and the planet we need.
Earth is the only home that we know;
If we destroy it there's no place else for us to go.
We're killing species of plants and animals,
Soon the Earth will be a republic of insects and grass.
The ozone layer is rapidly depleting;
Our life-giving sun might just kill us through heating.
We're using up our resources incredibly fast;
We're naïve if we actually believe they will last.
We're polluting the land and the sea and the air;
Soon there won't be a clean place to live anywhere.
In short it seems clear that our planet will die;
But if you won't accept this then neither will I.
So think about the consequences of the actions you take,
And remember the difference one person can make.

Farah Mahmood (13)
Selly Park Technology College

The Environment

It's all foggy now, I can't even see,
The smoke is all around, choking me.
The cars go past without a care,
They don't understand that it's not fair.

My stem is tilted,
My petals are falling,
I'm nearly there,
Death is calling.

Then I think, I'm saved as I start to see some rain.
Then I feel it burn holes through my leaves, and think,
Here comes the pain!
The air used to be clean, fresh and clear,
Now I stand still, rigid with fear.

I feel dizzy, my head is spinning.
I'm playing a game and there's no winning.
Where's my friends, my family, my peers?
As I reminisce, I can feel tears.

I hear a crack, in my stem, I feel a bend,
Now I know, this is the end.

Rahima Begum (12)
Selly Park Technology College

Pollution

Pollution, pollution everywhere,
In your homes and in the air.
Have a go at cleaning our world,
For you, me and them all around.
The more transport and gases that we use
Causes a bigger carbon footprint, so what should we choose?
Cars, trains and aeroplanes
All let out gases,
So let's save the world
In big masses.

Francesca Emery (11)
Selly Park Technology College

Think Of The Earth

Don't waste food.
Don't leave the tap running.
Think of the Earth.

Don't throw papers on the street.
Don't kick that rubbish with your feet.
Don't ask me to love you.
Think of the Earth.

Don't throw the rubbish in the grass.
Don't shout out in lessons.
Don't call out the answers in the lessons.
Think of the Earth.

Don't waste the light.
Don't eat in the street and throw the rubbish away.
Play sports all the time.
Think of the Earth.

Don't mistreat the animals.
Don't throw away your clothes.
Think of the Earth.
Think of the Earth.

Aisha Slem
Selly Park Technology College

A Better Place

Dreaming of a better world,
Fresher air and greener fields,
Sorting paper, plastic, glass -
All things to recycle fast.
Little things can make big changes,
For a better life through the ages.
Make the world a better place.

Shannon McCleary (11)
Selly Park Technology College

Could You Imagine?

Could you imagine life without school?
You couldn't learn or be cool.
Could you imagine not seeing grass?
We could not see the land's mass.
Could you imagine life without mammals?
You wouldn't see the distinct animals.
No more searching, seeking and investigating,
For that one special place,
We would lose the human race,
Earth would become boiling hot,
Like a sizzling pot.
All the cool, brisk air would be gone,
We would not see dusk or dawn.
Glaciers would liquefy,
Antarctica would melt and we'd say bye-bye.
We can help now,
Anyway you know how!

Sabah Razaq (13)
Selly Park Technology College

What's The Point?

What's the point in all this war?
The world can't take it anymore.
All the suffering, all the pain,
Why do we do it?
It's just insane.

Lives are lost every day,
All families do is pray and pray
To get their loved ones back alive,
After all the bombs, hoping they survive.

We are all equal,
We are all the same,
So what's the point
In causing this pain?

Natalie Cooper (14)
Smestow School

Our World Through Different Eyes

You see it in the news,
You read it in the paper,
Everything will change,
Think about it now not later.

I know it is hard
Acting all green,
But there is loads to do,
Don't just moan and scream.

From recycling to war
And racism to hate,
Pollution will fight against us
Act now before it's too late.

Animals will get extinct,
Rainforests will die out,
Poverty will take over,
It may be the last time you see a trout.

Don't you care?
Can't you see
This our fault
Even me.

I'm trying my hardest
To make this right.
You could all help
Keep it in the light.

We need to work together
And fight this forever.
Don't you care?
Don't you see
The world is dying
Can we get through this?
Hmmm, maybe.

Fiona Stebbing (12)
Smestow School

Make Peace Not War!

Why are we fighting?
We should be making peace.
Why are we fighting?
Can we stop this please?

Why are we fighting?
Is this for the best?
Why are we fighting?
Why can't we just rest?

We should have peace
And try to forget war.
We should have peace,
Shall I tell you more?

We should stop the war
And make more peace.
We should stop the war,
Don't you agree?

So just think about this war,
How'd you feel if you lost everything you had?
But you could've done something to stop that war,
That's why I say, make peace not war!

Jochebed Asiedu (13)
Smestow School

The Homeless Man

I came to the big city for fame and money,
All I have is this cardboard box
And a nose that's runny,
I walk the streets from dusk till dawn,
When I came here I hoped for a house with a lawn,
So if you think of the big city just like me,
Stay where you are with a house,
A lawn, with a warm cup of tea
Coz all I have is this box and these clothes,
No house, no lawn just a cold runny nose.

Charlie Kelly (14)
Smestow School

War Is Coming

A war is coming soon,
With your AK47s
And your carbine rifles too.

You pop each other's heads open,
Like one big fat watermelon,
Why can't you all be
Nice and sign a treaty?

A war is coming soon,
With your AK47s,
And your carbine rifles too.

Your sons and daughters and your wives,
They don't know if you're alive.
You could be dead without a head,
Like the news has once said.

A war is coming soon,
With your AK47s,
And your carbine rifles too.

Connor Woods (12)
Smestow School

War

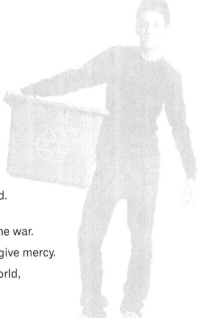

War, war is a bore,
It makes people really poor.

War, war is really sore,
It makes people really poor.

War, war is really sad,
They don't know it's really bad.

Guns, guns are really hurting,
Because they are hurting in the war.

Mercy, mercy, why can't they give mercy.

Guns, guns are hurting the world,
Please stop this hated war.

Paramdeep Panesar (12)
Smestow School

Start Now!

Recycling is easy,
Recycling is fun,
Even when it's breezy,
It's just not sleazy,
Don't make it uneasy
And stop being cheesy.

Get that tin,
Put it in the bin.

Twirled in a world
Where recycling is in need,
Don't smoke weed,
Do a good deed
Because the world is in need.

Don't be bitter
And drop your litter.
You don't have to sin,
Put it in the bin!

Kellyanne Davenport (14)
Smestow School

What Is Green?

What is green?
Green is life.
Green is a colour
That keeps us alive.

What is green?
Green is trees.
Trees are alive
Like you and me.

Trees are paper.
Paper can waste.
If you waste the paper
You're destroying the environment race.

Kamran Basran (12)
Smestow School

Green Is The Key!

Thirty degrees
Will keep you at ease
Just watch your bills increase

Climate change
Obviously feels strange
Cos it could drive you deranged

Racism, is not allowed
It does not make you feel proud
Bullying will never join a crowd

Poverty is not alright
You wouldn't be able to hear the sight
Losing something you own could get into fights

Your Earth needs you
In order to keep it new
For you and all your fellow crew!

Christine Yu (14)
Smestow School

War

A war is coming now,
I don't know how,
Why can't there be a sign of peace?
Drop your weapons at least.

People might die,
Their loved ones cry,
Don't shoot the gun,
Go and have some fun.

Go back to base,
And pack your suitcase,
Go and stay at home,
Leave the war alone!

Jacob Bull (12)
Smestow School

The Silent War

People dying,
More crying,
People dying,
More sighing.

So what is all this fighting for?
Is there really any need for war?

The ones we have lost through hate and debate,
Were treated like a piece of bait.

Why continue war?
Do we really need anymore?

Think of all the hurt and pain,
Will this always carry on the same?

Please help stop war,
There is no need for anymore!

Katie Pawlowski (12)
Smestow School

Our World

Afghanistan, Iran, Iraq,
All we want is our troops back.
War is chaos, stop,
Please live in peace.
The whole world just wants to be safe,
Guns, bombs, knives and hate,
All in one it makes the world unsafe.
Fighting for us or for the state?
Blood and guts on the roads,
More war supplies in lorry loads.
Rotting bones,
Frightened people all alone.
This is no way for anyone to live,
Countries need help, let's give it.
Ceasefire, *no* stop the war altogether
And leave it like that forever.

Ciaran Charlesworth (12)
Smestow School

What Is War For?

What is war?
War is disagreement,
War is loss of lives,
War is a waste of money,
War is blood,
What is war?

What is war for?
War is for your country,
War is for power,
War is for victory,
War is for honour,
What is war for?

Ryan Ahir (14)
Smestow School

The Homeless Are Coming?

The homeless are coming,
Coming they are.
They come and they come
But we don't care.

They sleep on streets
And live under bridges
And beg for our food from our fridges.

They just stay while we do nothing,
Something must be done, just something.
If they could all get jobs to keep off the streets
They could pay for their own upkeep.

Lauren Dudley (12)
Smestow School

Animal Life

The animals in our world
Have a right to live.

The tusks on an elephant stand proud and white
But also on a poacher's wall.

The cheetahs are calm, they run so fast,
The people are calm, they look so cool in a cloak.

The whales swim for their own freedom,
The people will eat for their own hunger.

The animals swim, run and stay,
If people keep with the promises they say.

Josh Wythe (12)
Smestow School

Pollution Keeps On Going

Pollution starts without you knowing,
And soon enough it won't be snowing.
The air we breathe is no longer fresh,
How can we let our world be such a mess?

If you don't get up and do something,
Our lives will be a mess . . .
Our children's children probably won't exist.

Think about being green not about being mean,
After all our world is a great place
So maybe change your mind about not being a disgrace.

Leonie Woolley (12)
Smestow School

The World's Mother

We don't own the world,
The world owns us.
We are but a pawn in Mother Nature's game,
So feel the shame.
Save the world, join together,
It won't be here forever.
Our love we'll share
And show we care.
I can't do it alone,
So help me!

Grace Wylde (12)
Smestow School

Feed The Homeless

Feed the homeless,
Don't make them boneless,
Stay awake and please, please bake.

Give them a home
So they won't be alone.
Buy them a ted
So they can stay snug up in bed.

Sticks and stones may break your bones,
So just give them a little bit of a loan.

Olivia Gooding (12)
Smestow School

128

Why?

Why do they discriminate?
Why do they judge me?
Why do I hurt so much?
Why do I live?

Why do they hate?
Why am I judged as a criminal?
Why don't they let it go?
Why do I live?

Shaquille Spence (14)
Smestow School

Litter!

Most people do not care
If they litter everywhere.
You see litter all on the streets
And chewing gum on people's feet.
Why don't they put it in the bin
Instead of dropping it while they are walking,
Or keep it in their pocket
And make a cool litter rocket?

Adam Tinsley (14)
Smestow School

Time

Time is a gift
Time is a waste
Sometimes you have too much
Sometimes not enough
Global warming is here
And it is here to stay
This could be prevented
By the way you live your day.

Luke Gilbert (14)
Smestow School

Pollution Panic

Polluting the air,
Wouldn't be fair,
For the world's a great big place,
So why not give up all the hate.
If we work together,
The world could last forever,
And we could live in harmony.
Let's save our world.

Florence Marsh (12)
Smestow School

War

War!
What is the point?
What do we gain
Apart from pain?
War!
What is the point?

Will Powell (14)
Smestow School

Litter Everywhere

Step out of the house, there it is,
The rubbish on the ground, 'it's taking the mick'.
What is wrong with people, there're bins all around,
But instead they think it easier to throw it on the ground.
Can't they see the mess that they have done?
It's done so often it's like the only way to have fun.

Siobhan Walker (14)
Smestow School

Poem To The Planet

Save our planet,
Save our trees,
Help the world
And save the seas.

Want to save a tiger?
Want to save a bear?
Send us an adoption form
To show that you care.

Save our planet,
Save our trees,
Help the world
And save the seas.

Want to save the flowers?
Want to save the trees?
Recycle your rubbish
And save whales in the seas.

Save our planet,
Save our trees,
Help the world
And save the seas.

Want to save the world?
Want to be green?
Then save the planet
And don't be mean.

Save our planet,
Save our trees,
Help the world
And save the seas.

Georgie Smith (12)
Summerhill Secondary School

Mother Nature

Her eyes made up of tiny, dainty petals,
Her lips made up of green leaves.
Her hair yellow strands of straw,
Her eyebrows made up of thin blades of grass.
Her wrinkles deepening each day.

Her heart made up of poor, homeless children,
Her lungs filled with black clouds of pollution.
Her liver made up of empty wrappers,
Her stomach bubbling with anger,
Every time there's racism for no reason.

Her worries of more animals becoming extinct,
Her worries of climate change.
Her worries of wars never stopping,
Her worries of everyone stopping recycling
Are making her sick at the thought.

As she's slowly becoming weaker,
Her last words seem to say:
'Look after the world,
If you don't it's gone forever.'
She lies there on a bed of petals.

She will never be forgotten,
As her spirit shall live on.
And her wise words,
Can be heard in the breeze,
That soft, gentle whisper . . .

Ellie Yates (11)
Summerhill Secondary School

My Greenie

What about war,
We don't need more.
What about global warming
There won't be a morning.

What about trust,
Help the world, we must,
What about understanding,
Not demanding.

Think, think, think.

What about crime,
Shouldn't we mime?
Stop diseases,
Keep the trees.

What about education,
Get well with medication,
What about cycling,
Why don't we start recycling?

Think, think, think.

What about gas,
Why do we throw away glass?

Think, think, think, think.

Help the world now!

Aaran Taylor (11)
Summerhill Secondary School

Recycling The World

What about girls?
What about boys?
What do you think about things?
What about dreams?
What about love?
What about things that we all do?

It's time to make our world change.
It's time to help our world.

Think about animals.
Think about people.
Think about children.
Think about all the things that we have done.
Think about people who have cancer.

It's time to make our world change.
It's time to help our world.

What about us?
What about babies?
What about people crying?
What about cats?
What about dogs?
What about animals dying?

It's time to make our world change.
It's time to help our world.

Hayley Turnbull (11)
Summerhill Secondary School

Why?

T hink hard what we have done to our world.
H ave we tried to help or do we sit at home?
E ventually the world is going to die, do we care?

W here are our souls?
O ur consciences are telling us but are we listening?
R ainforests are dying, do we care?
L ack of education, do we care?
D isease and suffering, do we care?

N obody cares.
E arth is dying!
E arth is dying!
D isease is spreading.
S till we do nothing. Think what we could do to help.

Y our money shared to people who have nothing.
O ur clothes to charity.
U nique people to help.
R esolutions we can keep.

H elp is on hand, you are our only hope!
E arth needs you!
L ives you could save and people you could help.
P lanet Earth needs you!

Eleanor Jane Cooper (11)
Summerhill Secondary School

Save Our Fantastic World

We have such a fantastic world,
But why don't we care a bit?
If we would think more carefully
Our world won't be a tip!

We can be so selfish!
There's starving children in need,
Stop thinking about yourself,
And cut down on the greed!

We have rainforests disappearing!
And trees being cut down,
Try and stop this happening!
Make the trees smile not frown!

Car fumes cause pollution,
Which is very bad for health,
If you use public transport
You'll be doing good for yourself.

We have such a fantastic world
Which you will now help to save.
If you use my instructions
The world will not turn to a grave!

Tom Freeman (11)
Summerhill Secondary School

Go On A Mission

Go on a mission,
To cut your carbon emission,
Make it your ambition,
To make this a tradition,
Turn off lights,
Use less heating on warmer nights,
This will cut your bill
And you will feel a great thrill,
So remove all clutter,
Be an emission cutter.

George Rogers (11)
Summerhill Secondary School

How And Why?

How do we stop poverty?
How do we help the trees?
We have come so far,
Why now, it's our turn,
We should understand
And love our world,
To help it be a better place,
Our planet is diseased,
We should build our trust
And work together that's all it takes,
Just one bit of trust,
To help our terrain,
Pollution is building,
What else can we do?
So, take the time to think,
Don't sit around,
Let's hop on our feet
And rise to the challenge,
So remember that our world is dying
As you can plainly see,
So help the world from poverty.

Chloe Smith (11)
Summerhill Secondary School

Just Think

Dream, oh how I dreamed,
I wanted to see how life was somewhere else.
But now I know what has happened. Just think.
I always thought the 6 o'clock news could bring some entertainment,
But guns and drugs have crawled upon us
And I don't know where peace is anymore. Just think.
The forests will not be here, animals will become extinct. Just think.
Disease is everywhere, people with no clothes, people with no jobs.
Just think.
We need to regain people's trust, we should think for us.
For the people around us and our world, just think.

Jessica Simms (11)
Summerhill Secondary School

What's Happening To Our World?

What happened to the forests,
The sun, the wind and the rain?
What happened to some animals,
The war, the hurt and the pain?
What's happen to our world?
Can you hear the children crying,
In the empty street?
Can you see their bare feet hurting,
No shoes upon their feet?
What's happening to our world?
What about all the intimidating fear
That spreads so far and wide?
As they sit so lonely in their homes
No one in which to confide.
What's happening in our world?
Imagine, if we understood each other
Wouldn't the world be a better place?
No hurt upon other people's faces,
Nothing bad, no disgrace.
What's happening to our world?

Mairead McNicholas (11)
Summerhill Secondary School

Why Is Our Life This Way?

What about poverty, suffering and war,
Where did this start?
Can't we all just get along?
Most of the world involved in crime!
Hatred and disease,
It happens all the time.

We are tearing our own world apart,
Can't we all change?
Global warming is rising up the chart,
So can't we all recycle, share and trust?
Let's all respect the environment
For the love of mankind.

Luke Duckworth (12)
Summerhill Secondary School

Stop And Think!

Stop!
Think about what you are doing,
Are you harming this world?

Think about the creatures,
Are they becoming extinct?
Think about pollution,
Are you putting lives on the brink?

Think about the rainforests,
Are you wasting trees?
Think about global warming,
Are you listening to our pleas?

Think about your household rubbish,
Are you recycling all you can?
Think about the landfill sites,
Please, please give us a helping hand.

Stop and think, you can play your part,
The time you finish reading this poem,
Is the time to start.

Abbigale Williams (11)
Summerhill Secondary School

We Can Help The World

W hy hurt our world where we live
E ven though we have love to give?

C an we keep doing this?
A nother chance we cannot miss.
N ow is the time to change our ways!

H arming the world just for greed,
E very day another bad deed.
L ife will end if we keep wanting more,
P eople will end up poor!

T ime to change for the good,
H eal the world as it should.
E veryone, it is time to change our ways!

W ill you join us before everything dies?
O pen your mind and use your eyes.
R evive our planet for our children's sake.
L earn to give and not to take.
D o it now, it is time to change our ways!

Emma Marsh (11)
Summerhill Secondary School

Think About The World

What about the girls?
What about the boys?
What about the twirls?
What about the toys?

I think about the bees,
I think about the trees,
Think about the animals' homes,
All the animals will be on their own.
Stop!
Remember the war,
We don't want it anymore,
Take one minute to look at the fresh blue sky,
We don't want it to die.

Sydney Griffiths (12)
Summerhill Secondary School

140

Why Is The World This Way?

What happened to the animals?
Where are the butterflies and the bees?
What has happened to the trees?

Why is the world this way?

What about the children
Who sleep in the rain?
Why must they suffer the pain?

Why is the world this way?

What about the world,
Is it slowly coming to an end?
We need to reduce the energy we spend!

Why is the world this way?

Imagine a better, happier place,
With smiling children, no obvious despair,
Trusting each other is the best way for the world to repair.

Hannah Fellows (11)
Summerhill Secondary School

Almost Outta Time!

What has happened to the world?
We should all love each other,
Like sister and brother.
We need to have faith in the world,
But what should we do?

If we work together we can make a change,
Everyone in their own special way.
We can solve our issues before the Earth starts to age.
We can save the world.

All we need is one act of random kindness at a time,
But time is short and the world isn't going to give us another sign.

We're almost outta time!

Ryan Taylor (11)
Summerhill Secondary School

The Planet

What about the rainforests?
What about the animals?
Why is the ice melting?
Why so much pollution?

What about the car exhausts?
What is your carbon footprint?
Why do people litter?
Why do they have to drive?

What about the children?
What about their food?
Why are they so hungry?
Why do they have to die?

What about our planet?
What about our future?
Why are there wars?
Why do people cry?

Peter Holmes (11)
Summerhill Secondary School

Life On Earth

Forests cut down for resources,
Cities infested with crime.
The polluted world will be ruined,
It's only a matter of time.

We can stop children from starving,
They cannot die anymore.
If we can stop causing pollution,
The Earth will not rot to the core.

The Earth is running out of patience,
Be careful what you throw away.
We have to change for the whole wide world,
But it will take more than a day.

Joshua Harris (11)
Summerhill Secondary School

Keep The World The Same

What about the trees?
We need the sunrise.
We need our lovely seas.
Keep our world the same.

What about the flowers?
Love our creatures.
Stop the pollution.
Keep our world the same.

What about starving children?
Stop the global warming.
What about disease?
Keep our world the same.

What about education?
We need to save our bees.
Love our planet, don't hunt it.
Keep our world the same.

Charlotte Marks (11)
Summerhill Secondary School

Earth And Life

Whatever happened to happiness?
Why are there wars?
Why are there people still starving,
Homeless and lying on floors.

What about respect for our environment?
Why do people pollute?
Why is there lack of education?
Why aren't there jobs to suit?

So, please help save our planet,
Be green and help those in need.
Help protect our surroundings
And help plants to self-seed.

Jack McHugh (11)
Summerhill Secondary School

Help Save The World

What about poverty?
What about starving kids?
What about the rainforest?
What about the trees?

Think about love.
Think about respect.
Think about sharing.
Think about giving all the best.

Stop all the crime.
Stop all the pollution.
Stop all disease.
Stop all the wars.

What about trust?
Think of recycling.
Stop global warming.
Help save the world!

Oliver Denning (11)
Summerhill Secondary School

Make A Difference

What about our world?
Do you even care?
Stop all the wars,
What is there to gain?

Give all people hospitality,
Give them all food,
Can't you understand
Everyone's pain?

Let's save the rainforest,
We've got paper to burn.
Make this madness
The past!

If we all join in
We can make a difference.
So everyone join in
And make that difference!

Tom Payne (11)
Summerhill Secondary School

Our World

Did you know that a bus can hold the same amount of people
as forty cars?
And it saves money and the cost of fuel.
I can recycle a plastic bottle, did you know it can power a light bulb for six
hours!
If you turn the tap off when you clean your teeth the saved water can fill an
Olympic pool!
We can stop the war, we need no more!
And we should recycle paper, or at least draw on both sides, that way the birds
and bees will have a home.
We need no more crime, if you don't have the time,
don't do the crime!
Reduce, reuse and recycle! Reduce, reuse and recycle!
Reduce, reuse and recycle!
Our world can change just you wait! We can: reduce, reuse and recycle, no
littering, sharing, giving and helping. Stop using up all of the things that are
going, going and soon will be gone.

Eleanor Corns (11)
Summerhill Secondary School

Young Writers
Information

We hope you have enjoyed reading this book - and that you will continue to enjoy it in the coming years.

If you like reading and writing poetry drop us a line, or give us a call, and we'll send you a free information pack.

Alternatively if you would like to order further copies of this book or any of our other titles, then please give us a call or log onto our website at www.youngwriters.co.uk

Young Writers Information
Remus House
Coltsfoot Drive
Peterborough
PE2 9JX
(01733) 890066